Moroccan
BIBLE

Moroccan

BIBLE

Rachael Lane

Contents

Introduction

In Morocco, the pleasure of eating food is equal to the pleasure of sharing it. Moroccan hospitality is evident from the moment you set foot inside a family home. After a warm greeting, you may even receive a dousing of perfume or scented water. Meanwhile, family members will be busy finishing their final preparations for the feast to come.

In this book there are more than 120 inspiring recipes to help you create your own Moroccan feasts. You can try simple grilled kebabs or the lavish, celebratory chicken bastilla. Make your own succulent tagines and piles of fluffy couscous covered with mouth-watering stews, as well as cleansing soups and salads, seafood and meat dishes, and tempting selections of Moroccan sweets. Extras include classic Moroccan flavourings, preserved lemons and harissa paste, and to conclude your feast, the traditional method for preparing mint tea.

Moroccan Basics

Morocco borders the Atlantic Ocean and the Mediterranean Sea. In the coastal regions fish and seafood can be found in abundance. The more fertile land is in the north, where the majority of citrus and other fruits, nuts and olives are grown. The south is more arid as a result of the Sahara desert with few crops being grown there.

Moroccan cuisine has been influenced over the centuries by the indigenous, mainly Muslim, Berber population. Spanish, Portuguese, French, Moorish, Middle Eastern, Mediterranean and African influences are also present and have helped shape the cuisine.

Main Ingredients

The marketplace is at the heart of Moroccan cuisine. These open-air stalls are alive with the fragrance of fresh herbs and pungent spices, the clatter of tea glasses on silver trays and eye-catching displays of intricately painted tagines and serving dishes, not to mention piles of gleaming fresh produce. The food section has everything a Moroccan kitchen needs, from fresh, dried and preserved produce to meat, poultry and fish. Other treats include large bullet-shaped cones of compacted sugar sold in bulk for sweetening mint tea, Chinese green tea, bottles of scented rose- and orange-blossom waters and tubs of wild honey.

As the Moroccan market shows, the key to Moroccan cooking is 'fresh is best'. The ingredients used in the recipes that follow are available from fresh food markets and specialist food stores. Alternative ingredients are suggested for the more unusual items.

VEGETABLES AND FRUIT

A bountiful array of fresh and seasonal produce is used in Moroccan cooking. The most widely used vegetables and fruits are red onions, tomatoes, root vegetables (such as potatoes, sweet potatoes, turnips and carrots), artichokes, okra, various types of lettuce, citrus fruits, red and green grapes, and stone fruits such as peaches, plums and nectarines.

HERBS

Fresh herbs are used in abundance, particularly flat-leaf parsley and coriander, and mint for making tea – if fresh mint is not available, sometimes dried mint is used.

MEAT, POULTRY AND SEAFOOD

Meat, poultry and seafood are used in tagine and couscous dishes, and special occasions may include a course of stuffed or slow-roasted meat, poultry or fish. Meat is often minced to make kefta for kebabs, or to fill briouats or fried breads. Most commonly eaten are chicken, lamb and mutton, goat, and beef. In the south it is common for camel to be eaten as well. Since Morocco is a Muslim country, pork is not seen on the menu, and all meat is halal in accordance with Islamic law.

DRY GOODS

Essential dry goods in Moroccan cooking include: semolina grains for making couscous, pastries and breads; chickpeas; lentils; dried beans, especially broad beans and green beans; rice; dried fruits such as dates, figs, raisins, apricots and prunes; and nuts and seeds such as almonds, sesame seeds, walnuts and peanuts.

SPICES AND FLAVOURINGS

Moroccan cooking is characterised by its fresh, zesty and spicy flavours. Essential to this are green, black and purple olives; preserved lemons; fiery red harissa paste; chermoula paste; and fruity olive oils.

The spicing of Moroccan cuisine is always subtle, not overpowering – spices are even used in sweet dishes. The main spices used are cumin, ginger, paprika, turmeric, black pepper, saffron, chilli, star anise, cinnamon and nutmeg.

There are four spice mixes that are commonly used as bases for tagine sauces. These are also used to flavour roast meats or couscous. They are:

- k'dra – a pale-yellow sauce made from butter, onion, saffron, white pepper and ground ginger

- m'charmel – a mixture of other sauces, generally red in colour, which often contains saffron, black pepper, red chilli, ground ginger and cumin
- m'hammer – a red sauce based on butter, paprika and cumin
- m'qualli – a yellow sauce containing ground ginger, saffron and oil

Cooking & Equipment

When buying a tagine dish, ensure you choose the appropriate one for your requirements. Some tagines, particularly the highly ornate ones, are designed for presentation only. The cooking vessels are made to withstand the heat of hot coals, the stove top and the oven.

If you don't have a tagine cooking vessel, it is still possible to make a tagine. Simply use a flameproof or ovenproof dish. Follow the recipe's instructions and cook on the stove top or in the oven at a low–medium temperature for approximately the same amount of time.

In Morocco, a couscoussier (a large pot consisting of two sections) is traditionally used for cooking couscous. A steamer saucepan can be used instead with satisfactory results. Line the perforated steamer base with muslin cloth to prevent the small couscous grains from falling into the broth below. Or fit a colander over a pot and seal the outer edges with foil to ensure the steam only escapes upwards to cook the couscous.

There is quite a knack to preparing couscous in the traditional Moroccan way. Grains are gently steamed, separated and dried, and the process is repeated, before the couscous is served with its accompanying broth or stew. Follow the instructions for traditional couscous on page 54 or, if time is short, use instant couscous – directions are on the packet.

Starters

Ever-popular kebabs and keftas can be seen cooking over hot coals at open-air restaurants and markets throughout Morocco. They are sold as snacks and starters, stuffed into bread and sometimes accompanied by a spicy tomato sauce or salsa. At home they make a perfect light lunch or addition to a barbecue.

Try making other popular Moroccan snacks, such as Cumin-spiced Chickpeas (page 26), which are traditionally sold in the evening in little paper cones. Briouats (fried pastries filled with lamb or tuna) are another tasty snack or a great start to a Moroccan feast.

❮ Beef Kefta Kebabs (page 12)

Beef Kefta Kebabs

Makes 10

750 g (1 lb 10 oz) beef mince

1 small onion, grated

2 tablespoons finely chopped
fresh flat-leaf parsley

2 tablespoons finely chopped
fresh coriander

2 teaspoons paprika

2 teaspoons ground cumin

½ teaspoon cayenne pepper

½ teaspoon salt

¼ teaspoon freshly ground
black pepper

If using bamboo skewers, soak them in cold water for 30 minutes to prevent them from burning. Alternatively, use metal skewers.

To make the keftas, place all the ingredients in a medium-sized bowl and mix well to combine. Divide the mixture into 10 even-sized portions. Shape into oval sausages and insert skewers through the centre, pressing firmly to secure. Place on a tray and refrigerate for 1 hour or until firm.

Preheat barbecue grill to high.

Grill the keftas for 3–5 minutes on each side or until cooked to your liking.

Fish Kebabs

Makes 8

600 g (1 lb 5 oz) hapuka or other firm white fish fillets, cut into 2.5-cm (1-in) cubes

CHERMOULA PASTE

3 cloves garlic, chopped

2 fresh hot red chillies, deseeded and chopped

½ bunch fresh coriander, leaves chopped

½ bunch fresh flat-leaf parsley, leaves chopped

¼ cup (60 ml/2 fl oz) olive oil

¼ cup (60 ml/2 fl oz) freshly squeezed lemon juice

1½ teaspoons paprika

1 teaspoon ground cumin

1 teaspoon ground coriander

½ teaspoon freshly ground black pepper

½ teaspoon salt

To make the chermoula, place the garlic, chilli, coriander and parsley in a food processor and blend to a paste. Add the olive oil, lemon juice, spices and salt, and blend to combine. Mix the fish and chermoula in a large bowl and toss to coat. Cover and place in the refrigerator to marinate for at least 6 hours or overnight.

If using bamboo skewers, soak them in cold water for 30 minutes to prevent them from burning. Alternatively, use metal skewers.

Preheat barbecue grill to high. Thread fish onto skewers and grill for 2 minutes on each side, until cooked.

Chicken Kebabs

Makes 8

600 g (1 lb 5 oz) skinless
  chicken breast fillets

1½ tablespoons (30 ml/1 fl oz)
  olive oil

juice of ½ lemon

¼ cup finely chopped fresh
  coriander

2 cloves garlic, crushed

2 teaspoons paprika

1 teaspoon ground ginger

½ teaspoon ground turmeric

½ teaspoon salt

¼ teaspoon freshly ground
  black pepper

Trim the chicken of any excess fat and cut into 2.5-cm (1-in) cubes.

Combine all of the ingredients in a medium-sized bowl and toss to coat.
Cover and place in the refrigerator to marinate for at least 6 hours or
overnight.

If using bamboo skewers, soak them in cold water for 30 minutes to prevent them from burning. Alternatively, use metal skewers.

Preheat barbecue grill to high.

Thread the chicken onto skewers and grill for 3–4 minutes on each side,
until cooked.

Sardine Keftas

Makes 16

1 kg (2 lb 3 oz) fresh sardines

2 tablespoons fine soft
   breadcrumbs

¼ cup (60 ml/2 fl oz) olive oil

CHERMOULA PASTE

1 clove garlic, chopped

1 tablespoon finely chopped
   fresh coriander

1 tablespoon finely chopped
   fresh flat-leaf parsley

1 tablespoon (20 ml/¾ fl oz)
   olive oil

1 tablespoon (20 ml/⅔ fl oz)
   freshly squeezed lemon juice

1 teaspoon paprika

1 teaspoon ground cumin

1 teaspoon ground coriander

¼ teaspoon freshly ground
   black pepper

½ teaspoon salt

To make the chermoula, place the garlic, coriander and parsley in a food processor and blend to a paste. Add the olive oil, lemon juice, spices and salt, and blend to combine.

Clean the sardines, removing the heads, tails and bones. Coarsely chop the flesh and pass through a mouli or mincer, or finely chop in a food processor.

Combine the sardine mince, chermoula paste and breadcrumbs in a bowl. Shape into plum-sized balls and flatten to create patties.

Heat the oil in a large non-stick frying pan over medium heat. Cook the patties for 3 minutes on each side, until browned and cooked through.

Lamb Briouats

Makes 20

2 tablespoons (40 ml/1½ fl oz) olive oil

1 medium-sized onion, grated

1 clove garlic, crushed

2 teaspoons ground cumin

2 teaspoons paprika

1 teaspoon ground cinnamon

½ teaspoon cayenne pepper

500 g (1 lb 2 oz) lamb mince

4 large eggs, lightly beaten, plus 1 egg yolk, lightly beaten

salt and freshly ground black pepper

10 spring roll wrappers

vegetable oil, for deep-frying

Heat the olive oil in a large frying pan over low–medium heat. Add the onion, garlic and spices, and cook until softened and fragrant. Add the mince and cook, stirring occasionally, for 3–5 minutes, until browned and just cooked through. Add the 4 beaten eggs and cook, stirring, for a further minute. Season with salt and pepper. Transfer to a medium-sized bowl and refrigerate for 30 minutes or until cooled.

Lay a spring roll wrapper on a clean bench and cut in half lengthways. Keep the remaining wrappers covered with cling wrap to prevent them from drying out.

Place a spoonful of filling at the end of each strip and fold it back and forth in triangles to create a triangular parcel. Brush the edges with a little egg yolk and press to seal. Repeat the process with the remaining filling and wrappers.

Heat vegetable oil to 180°C (360°F) in a large frying pan or until a small piece of bread browns in 15 seconds when tested.

Deep-fry the briouats in batches for 30–40 seconds on each side, until golden and crisp. Remove using a slotted spoon and drain on paper towel.

※ In Morocco, briouats are traditionally made with warka pastry. Warka pastry is difficult and time consuming to make and near impossible to buy outside of Morocco. Spring roll wrappers are the closest substitute.

Tuna Briouats

Makes 4

1 × 185-g (6½-oz) can tuna, drained

1 preserved lemon, skin finely chopped

½ small red onion, finely chopped

1 teaspoon cayenne pepper

2 tablespoons finely chopped fresh flat-leaf parsley

1 tablespoon finely chopped fresh coriander

salt and ground black pepper

cornflour, for dusting

4 spring-roll wrappers

4 small eggs, plus 2 egg yolks

vegetable oil, for deep-frying

Combine the tuna with the lemon, onion, cayenne pepper, herbs and the seasoning in a medium-sized bowl. Lightly dust your work surface with cornflour and lay a spring-roll wrapper on top. Cover remaining wrappers with cling wrap to prevent drying out. Place one-quarter of the filling in the centre of the wrapper. Make a well in the centre of the filling and crack an egg into it. Fold two of the edges into the centre, to cover the filling. Brush remaining edges with egg yolk and fold over to enclose the filling, pressing to seal. Repeat with remaining filling and wrappers.

Meanwhile, heat the oil to 180°C (360°F). As soon as they're assembled, deep-fry the briouats, in batches, for 20–30 seconds on each side. The egg yolk should still be runny in the centre. Remove and drain on paper towel.

Moroccan Calzone

Rghaif

Makes 10

olive oil, for frying

BEEF FILLING

2 tablespoons (40 ml/1½ fl oz)
olive oil

1 medium-sized onion, finely
chopped

2 tablespoons paprika

2 teaspoons ground cumin

1 teaspoon cayenne pepper

500 g (1 lb 2 oz) beef mince

salt and freshly ground black
pepper

DOUGH

3 cups (450 g/1 lb) plain flour

2 teaspoons salt

1 tablespoon (15 g/½ oz) dry
yeast

2 teaspoons caster sugar

1 cup (250 ml/8½ fl oz)
lukewarm water

To make the beef filling, heat the oil in a large frying pan over low–medium heat. Add the onion and spices, and cook until softened and fragrant. Add the mince and cook for 3–4 minutes, stirring occasionally, until browned. Pour in ⅓ cup (80 ml/3 fl oz) water and bring to the boil. Decrease the heat to low and gently simmer until the liquid has evaporated. Season with salt and pepper, and set aside to cool. >

To make the dough, combine the flour, salt, yeast and sugar in a medium-sized bowl. Gradually add the water, stirring, until a dough begins to form.

Knead the dough for 15–20 minutes, until it becomes a smooth elastic ball. With lightly oiled hands, shape the dough into 10 even-sized balls. Stretch and roll the dough out, one ball at a time, to make 20-cm (8-in) paper-thin squares.

Spread one-tenth of the filling in the centre of each square. Fold two opposite edges into the centre, overlapping to cover the filling. Then fold the remaining edges in, again overlapping, to completely encase the filling. Using your hands, flatten out the dough parcel to its original size. Transfer to a lightly oiled tray and put in a warm place to rise for 30–45 minutes or until doubled in size.

Heat a medium-sized frying pan over medium–high heat. Drizzle with oil and cook the parcels, one or two at a time, for 1–2 minutes on each side or until golden brown.

Spiced Lentils

Serves 6

2 tablespoons (40 ml/1½ fl oz) olive oil

1 small red onion, finely chopped

2 cloves garlic, finely chopped

1 teaspoon ground cumin

1 teaspoon paprika

4 tomatoes, peeled, deseeded and finely chopped

2 cups dried green or brown lentils

2 tablespoons finely chopped fresh flat-leaf parsley

2 tablespoons finely chopped fresh coriander

salt and freshly ground black pepper

Heat the oil in a large frying pan over low–medium heat. Add the onion, garlic, cumin and paprika and sauté until softened and fragrant.

Add the chopped tomato and cook for 3 minutes, until softened. Add the lentils and ½ cup (125 ml/4 fl oz) water and bring to the boil. Reduce the heat to low and cook for 8–10 minutes, until tender.

Stir in the parsley, coriander, and salt and pepper.

Cumin-spiced Chickpeas

Serves 4

1½ cups dried chickpeas

2 tablespoons (40 ml/1½ fl oz)
olive oil

1 tablespoon finely chopped
fresh coriander

1 tablespoon ground cumin

salt and freshly ground black
pepper

Soak the chickpeas in cold water for at least 6 hours or overnight.

Drain and rinse the chickpeas, and place in a medium-sized saucepan.
Cover with cold water and bring to the boil over high heat. Cook for 1 hour
or until tender. Drain and set aside.

Heat the oil in a large frying pan over low heat. Add the chickpeas, coriander and cumin and toss to coat. Season with salt and pepper. Drain on
paper towel.

❖ These chickpeas are a typical street food, usually served in paper cones.

❖ Dried broad beans can be prepared in the same way.

Fried Potato Cakes

Maakouda

Makes 10

3 medium-sized (450 g/1 lb)
  potatoes, washed

2 large eggs

2 tablespoons finely chopped
  fresh flat-leaf parsley

2 tablespoons finely chopped
  fresh coriander

2 teaspoons ground cumin

1 teaspoon paprika

¼ teaspoon ground turmeric

salt and freshly ground black
  pepper

vegetable oil, for frying

¼ cup (35 g/1¼ oz) plain flour

Place the unpeeled potatoes in a medium-sized saucepan and cover with cold water. Bring to the boil over high heat. Decrease the heat to medium and cook for 35–40 minutes, until tender. Drain and set aside to cool slightly. Peel the potatoes and mash or pass through a potato ricer.

Combine the potato with 1 egg and the herbs and spices in a bowl. Add salt and pepper. Shape into 10 even-sized balls and flatten to make patties.

Pour oil into a medium-sized frying pan to a depth of 2 cm (¾ in) and place over medium heat.

Lightly beat the remaining egg in a shallow bowl and place the flour in another. Dip the potato cakes into the egg, then lightly coat in flour. Cook for 2–3 minutes on each side, until golden brown. Drain on paper towel.

Soups & Salads

Soup, although generally not common in Morocco, plays a significant role in the Muslim month of Ramadan. During this festival, bowls of harira, considered to be the national soup, are made in endless variations and served at every family table at sundown to break the day's fast. A rich, nutritious soup filled with vegetables and pulses, harira is traditionally served alongside fresh dates, mounds of toasted slelou (sesame, almond and honey paste) and sweet, sticky pastries such as chebbakia and almond-filled briouats.

Most Moroccan meals begin with or are accompanied by an array of salads. These range from simple raw salads of orange and lettuce, or the popular Moroccan salad of tomato, cucumber and red onion, to slow-cooked bakkoula or spicy cauliflower salad.

‹ Harira Soup (page 32)

Harira Soup

Serves 8

450 g (1 lb) lamb shoulder
  chops

3 tablespoons (60 g/2 oz) butter

2 large onions, finely chopped

1 teaspoon ground turmeric

1 teaspoon freshly ground
  black pepper

½ teaspoon ground cinnamon

pinch of saffron threads,
  crushed

wings, neck, heart and liver
  of 1 chicken

1 cup finely chopped celery
  leaves

700-g (1 lb 9-oz) jar passata

¾ cup dried green or brown
  lentils

2 tablespoons tomato paste

2 tablespoons (30 g/1 oz)
  plain flour

small handful of vermicelli
  pasta

½ cup finely chopped fresh
  coriander

½ cup finely chopped fresh
  flat-leaf parsley

juice of 1 lemon

salt

Remove the lamb from the bones and cut the meat into 1.5-cm (⅝-in) cubes. Set the meat and bones aside.

Melt the butter in a large saucepan over low–medium heat. Add the onion and spices, and sauté until softened and fragrant. Add the lamb and bones, chicken pieces and celery leaves, and cook, stirring occasionally, for 15 minutes. Add the passata, lentils and tomato paste and stir together.

Pour in 1.5 L (3 pt 3 fl oz) water and bring to the boil. Decrease the heat to low and cook for 30–40 minutes, until the lentils are tender.

Combine the flour with the remaining water in a small bowl. Gradually pour the flour mixture into the hot soup, stirring continuously to prevent lumps. Gently simmer for 5 minutes.

Increase the heat and bring to the boil. Add the pasta, coriander, parsley and lemon juice. Cook, stirring occasionally, for 5–10 minutes, until the pasta is cooked. Season with salt.

❊ Harira is Morocco's most well-known soup. A highly nutritious soup with endless variations, it is eaten at sundown to break the fast throughout the month of Ramadan. It is traditionally served with dates, hard-boiled eggs and sweet pastries such as chebbakia (page 179) or almond briouats (page 182).

Broad Bean Soup

Beyssara

Serves 6

450 g (1 lb) dried broad beans

1.5 L (3 pt 3 fl oz) vegetable stock or water

5 cloves garlic, peeled

1½ teaspoons paprika, plus extra to garnish

1½ teaspoons ground cumin, plus extra to garnish

salt

drizzle of extra-virgin olive oil

Soak the broad beans in cold water overnight. Drain, rinse and skin the beans.

Place the beans, stock or water, garlic, paprika and cumin in a medium-sized saucepan and bring to the boil. (Do not add the salt at this stage as it will cause the beans to toughen.) Decrease the heat to low–medium and simmer for 1–1½ hours, until the beans are soft.

Purée the beans, the garlic and the cooking liquid together using a hand-held blender or food processor. Add a little more liquid if the mixture is too thick. Season with salt.

To serve, ladle the soup into bowls, drizzle with oil and sprinkle with paprika and cumin.

Aniseed & Semolina Soup

Serves 8

1½ cups (240 g/8½ oz) coarse
semolina

2 tablespoons (40 g/1½ oz)
butter

pinch of saffron threads,
crushed

3 cups (750 ml/25 fl oz) milk

2 teaspoons ground aniseed

salt and freshly ground black
pepper

Place 1.5 L (3 pt 3 fl oz) water in a medium-sized saucepan over medium–
high heat until hot, not boiling. Pour in the semolina in a thin stream,
stirring to prevent lumps. Add the butter and saffron, and bring to the boil.
Decrease the heat to low and cook for 20–30 minutes, until the semolina is
soft, swollen and cooked.

Meanwhile, heat the milk and aniseed together over low–medium heat,
until almost simmering. Add to the semolina and stir to combine. Season
with salt and pepper.

Caraway Soup

Serves 8

1.5 L (3 pt 3 fl oz) milk

120 g (4 oz) plain flour

2 tablespoons ground
caraway seeds

6–8 sprigs fresh mint

¼ cup (60 ml/2 fl oz) freshly
squeezed lemon juice

salt

Heat the milk together with 1.5 L (3 pt 3 fl oz) water and in a medium-sized saucepan over medium–high heat until hot, not boiling. Combine the flour with 2 cups (500 ml/ 17 fl oz) water in a medium-sized bowl. Gradually pour the flour mixture into the hot milk and water, whisking to prevent lumps.

Add the caraway and mint, and bring to the boil, stirring constantly. Decrease the heat to low and gently simmer for 5 minutes. Remove from the heat and set aside for 30 minutes to allow the flavours to infuse.

Strain the soup through a fine-mesh sieve to remove any lumps. Discard the mint.

Return the soup to the heat and gently bring to almost simmering point. Add the lemon juice, stirring to combine, and season with salt.

❈ This soup is traditionally served with steamed sheep's head.

Beetroot Salad

Serves 4

4 medium-sized beetroots

1½ tablespoons (30 ml/1 fl oz)
  olive oil

1 tablespoon (20 ml/¾ fl oz)
  freshly squeezed lemon juice

½ teaspoon ground cumin

salt

2 tablespoons finely chopped
  fresh coriander

Trim the stems off the beetroots and wash thoroughly. Place in a large saucepan, cover with water and bring to the boil over medium–high heat. Cook for 1 hour or until tender. Leave in the water to cool for 30 minutes.

Wearing food-handling gloves (to prevent staining your hands), peel the beetroots. Cut into bite-sized pieces and place in a medium-sized bowl.

Combine the olive oil, lemon juice and cumin in a small bowl. Pour the dressing over the beetroot and stir to coat. Season with salt and set aside for 1 hour to allow the flavours to develop.

Sprinkle with the fresh coriander and serve.

Spicy Potato Salad

Serves 4

¼ cup (60 ml/2 fl oz) olive oil

2 teaspoons paprika

2 teaspoons ground cumin

4 medium-sized potatoes, cut
into 2-cm (¾-in) cubes

2 tablespoons finely chopped
fresh flat-leaf parsley

2 tablespoons finely chopped
fresh coriander

salt and freshly ground
black pepper

Heat the oil in a large frying pan over medium heat. Add the spices and potato, and cook for 3–5 minutes, stirring occasionally, until golden.

Add ⅓ cup (80 ml/3 fl oz) water, then cover and cook over low heat for 10–15 minutes, until tender. Stir in the parsley, coriander, and salt and pepper.

Serve warm.

Potato & Capsicum Salad

Serves 4

2 tablespoons (40 ml/1½ fl oz) olive oil

2 cloves garlic, finely chopped

1 teaspoon ground turmeric

1 teaspoon paprika

½ teaspoon ground ginger

2 tomatoes, peeled, deseeded and coarsely chopped

2 green capsicums, deseeded and coarsely chopped

3 tablespoons finely chopped fresh coriander

⅓ cup (80 ml/3 fl oz) water

2 large potatoes, cut into 2-cm (¾-in) cubes

1 preserved lemon, deseeded and coarsely chopped

salt and freshly ground black pepper

Heat the oil in a large frying pan over low heat. Add the garlic and spices, and sauté until softened and fragrant. Add the tomato, capsicum, coriander and water. Cover and cook for 45 minutes.

Add the potato and lemon to the pan, cover and cook for a further 15 minutes. Uncover and cook for 20 minutes, stirring occasionally, until the liquid has evaporated and the potato is tender. Season with salt and pepper.

Serve warm or cold.

Sweet Carrot & Orange Salad

Serves 4

2 oranges, peeled

6 medium-sized carrots, grated

juice of ½ lemon

1 teaspoon orange-blossom water

2 tablespoons (30 g/1 oz) sugar

1½ teaspoons ground cinnamon, plus extra for dusting

pinch of salt

Using a small, sharp knife and working with a bowl underneath to catch any juice, cut the flesh out of each orange segment and place in a separate medium-sized bowl. Squeeze any remaining juice from the oranges into the bowl you were working over.

Add the carrot to the bowl with the orange segments.

Combine the reserved orange juice with the lemon juice, orange-blossom water, sugar, cinnamon and salt in a bowl. Pour the dressing over the salad and stir to combine. Refrigerate for 1 hour to allow the flavours to develop.

Serve chilled, sprinkled with cinnamon.

Cucumber Salad

Serves 4

6 Lebanese cucumbers, peeled
and deseeded

3 tablespoons (60 ml/2 fl oz)
olive oil

2 tablespoons (40 ml/1½ fl oz)
white-wine vinegar

1 tablespoon (15 g/½ oz)
caster sugar

1 tablespoon finely chopped
fresh thyme

salt

Coarsely grate the cucumber and drain off any excess liquid.

Combine the oil, vinegar, sugar and thyme in a small bowl. Add the grated cucumber and stir to combine. Season with salt and refrigerate until chilled.

Marshmallow Leaf Salad

Bakkoula

Serves 4

6 cups finely chopped spinach

1 cup finely chopped fresh flat-leaf parsley

¼ cup finely chopped fresh coriander

4 cloves garlic, peeled

2 teaspoons salt

2 teaspoons paprika

¼ cup (60 ml/2 fl oz) olive oil

¼ cup (60 ml/2 fl oz) lemon juice

1½ teaspoons ground cumin

¼ cup green olives

1 preserved lemon, quartered, flesh discarded and skin finely sliced

Place the spinach, parsley, coriander, garlic, salt and paprika in a large saucepan. Add ½ cup (125 ml/4 fl oz) water, cover and cook over low heat for 10 minutes, until tender. Add ¼ cup (60 ml/2 fl oz) water, stir, cover and cook for a further 2 hours.

Add the oil and cook, uncovered, for 20 minutes or until all the liquid has evaporated. Add the lemon juice and cumin, stir to combine and cook for a further 10–15 minutes, until all the liquid has evaporated. Transfer to a medium-sized bowl and refrigerate until chilled.

Serve garnished with olives and slices of preserved lemon.

❋ Marshmallow leaves can be difficult to find outside of Morocco. Here, spinach is used as a substitute.

Orange & Lettuce Salad

Serves 4

2 oranges

2 baby cos lettuces

2 tablespoons (40 ml/1½ fl oz)
   lemon juice

1 teaspoon orange-blossom
   water

1 tablespoon (20 ml/¾ fl oz)
   olive oil

2 teaspoons caster sugar

pinch of salt

Using a small, sharp knife, cut the flesh out of each orange segment and place in a medium-sized bowl.

Roughly tear the lettuce into small pieces and add to the bowl with the orange segments.

Combine the lemon juice, orange-blossom water, oil, sugar and salt in a small bowl. Pour the dressing over the salad and toss to combine.

Moroccan Salad

Serves 4

3 tomatoes, peeled, deseeded
and finely diced

1 Lebanese cucumber, peeled,
deseeded and finely diced

2 green capsicums, finely
diced

1 small red onion, finely diced

2 tablespoons (40 ml/1½ fl oz)
olive oil

juice of ½ lemon

salt and freshly ground black
pepper

Place the tomato, cucumber, capsicum and onion in a medium-sized bowl.

Mix the olive oil and lemon juice in a small bowl. Add to the vegetables and
stir to combine. Season with salt and pepper.

Spicy Cauliflower Salad

Serves 4

1 cauliflower, cut into large florets

2 tablespoons (40 ml/1½ fl oz) olive oil

2 cloves garlic, finely chopped

1 teaspoon ground turmeric

1 teaspoon paprika

2 tomatoes, peeled, deseeded and coarsely chopped

3 tablespoons finely chopped fresh coriander

¼ cup green olives

1 preserved lemon, deseeded and coarsely chopped

salt and freshly ground black pepper

Place the cauliflower in a medium-sized saucepan and cover with water. Place over medium–high heat and bring to the boil. Decrease the heat to low and cook for 2 minutes, then drain and set aside.

Heat the oil in a large frying pan over low heat. Add the garlic, turmeric and paprika and sauté until softened and fragrant. Add the tomato, coriander and ⅓ cup (80 ml/3 fl oz) water. Cover and simmer for 30 minutes.

Add the cauliflower, olives and lemon and cook for a further 20 minutes, stirring occasionally, until the liquid has evaporated and the cauliflower is tender. Season with salt and pepper.

Serve warm or cold.

Couscous

In Morocco, couscous refers not only to the swollen semolina granules but to the flavoursome stew and broth over which the granules are steamed. This combination creates one of Morocco's most famous dishes. Traditionally served on Friday, the main day of prayer, couscous is ever-present as the final course in celebratory feasts.

Packaged couscous is readily available in supermarkets, and is quick and easy to prepare. However, instant couscous cannot compare with the more time-consuming Moroccan dish. Fluffy and infused with the succulent flavours of meat, spices and vegetables, traditional Moroccan couscous is an absolute delight.

< Traditional Moroccan Couscous (page 54)

Traditional Moroccan Couscous

Serves 6

3 cups couscous
1 tablespoon salt
2 tablespoons (40 ml/1½ fl oz) olive oil

Step 1. Place the couscous in a large, deep tray. Mix the salt together with 1 L (34 fl oz) water in a large bowl. Sprinkle 1½ cups (375 ml/12½ fl oz) of the salted water over the couscous, rubbing it through with your fingers to separate the grains as you go. Set aside for 15 minutes to allow the grains to swell and dry out a little.

Step 2. Rub your fingers through the couscous again, breaking up any lumps. Place the couscous in the top of a steamer saucepan lined with muslin cloth and set over the simmering stew (see following recipes), ensuring that the steamer is not touching the liquid below. Cover and cook until steam begins to rise through the couscous, then cook for a further 10 minutes. Tip the couscous out into a large, deep tray, raking through the grains with your fingers or a spoon, and set aside to dry out a little. Gradually sprinkle with 1 cup (250 ml/8 fl oz) water, rubbing it through with your fingers and separating the grains. Drizzle with the oil and toss through to coat. Set aside for 15 minutes, to allow the grains to swell and dry out a little.

Step 3. Repeat the steaming, drying and raking process, then sprinkle couscous with another 1 cup (250 ml/8 fl oz) water. Set aside for 15 minutes to allow the grains to swell and dry out a little or, if preparing the couscous in advance, cover with a clean, damp cloth and set aside until required. The couscous can be kept at this stage for 3–4 hours.

Step 4. Rub your fingers through the couscous again, separating the grains and breaking up any lumps. Gradually sprinkle with the remaining water, rubbing it through with your fingers. Set aside for 15 minutes to allow the grains to swell and dry out a little. Place the couscous in the top of the steamer and steam for the third and final time over the simmering stew, or if the stew has finished cooking, steam over a saucepan of boiling water. Tip the couscous out into a large, deep tray. Rake the grains out flat, allowing the steam to rise and the couscous to dry out a little.

Serve with the accompanying stew and broth.

❊ If time is short, use instant couscous (available at supermarkets) and prepare it following the directions on the packet.

Seven-vegetable Couscous

Serves 6

1 quantity traditional
Moroccan couscous (page 54)

500 g–650 g (1 lb 2 oz–1 lb
7 oz) lamb shanks

¼ cup (60 ml/2 fl oz) olive oil

¼ cup (60 ml/2 fl oz) vegetable
oil

6 medium-sized tomatoes,
peeled

1 large red onion, sliced

1 tablespoon salt

2 teaspoons paprika

1½ teaspoons freshly ground
black pepper

1½ teaspoons ground turmeric

1½ teaspoons ground ginger

½ bunch fresh coriander,
washed and tied with
kitchen string

1 beef stock cube

4 medium-sized carrots, cut
in half across then in half
lengthways and cored

2–3 medium-sized turnips,
quartered

2–3 medium-sized potatoes,
cut in half lengthways

4 medium-sized zucchini, cut
in half across then in half
lengthways and deseeded

¼ small pumpkin, cut into
large chunks

1 fresh mild green chilli

Prepare the couscous using the traditional method or use instant couscous
and follow the directions on the packet.

Place the lamb, oils, 1 coarsely chopped tomato, the onion, salt, spices and coriander in the bottom of a large steamer saucepan. Cook over medium-high heat for 5–10 minutes, until the lamb is browned and the spices are fragrant.

Pour in enough water to just cover the lamb. Crumble in the stock cube, cover the pan and bring to the boil over high heat. Decrease the heat to low–medium, cover and simmer gently for 1 hour.

Meanwhile, prepare the vegetables. Cut the remaining tomatoes in half, remove and discard the seeds, and chop coarsely. Add the tomato, carrot, turnip and potato to the saucepan with the lamb and continue to simmer gently for 30 minutes.

Add the remaining vegetables and the chilli to the pan and simmer for a further 30 minutes, adding a little more water if necessary.

Pile the couscous onto a large serving plate, making a slight well in the centre. Arrange the vegetables around the outside of the couscous and spoon the stew into the centre, drizzling a little of the broth over the top. Place any remaining broth in a bowl, to be spooned over the couscous as desired.

Couscous with Veal & Raisins

Serves 6

1 quantity traditional
  Moroccan couscous (page 54)

2 tablespoons (40 ml/1½ fl oz)
  vegetable oil

100 g (3½ oz) butter

500 g (1 lb 2 oz) veal osso
  bucco

2 teaspoons ground cinnamon

1 teaspoon ground ginger

½ teaspoon ground turmeric

½ teaspoon ground cumin

pinch of saffron threads

½ teaspoon freshly ground
  black pepper

1 teaspoon salt

½ bunch fresh flat-leaf parsley,
  washed and tied with
  kitchen string

4 large red onions,
  thickly sliced

2 cloves garlic, finely chopped

3 tablespoons honey

1 cup raisins

Prepare the couscous using the traditional method or use instant couscous and follow the directions on the packet.

Heat the oil and half of the butter in the bottom of a large steamer saucepan. Add the veal, spices and salt, and cook over medium–high heat for 5–10 minutes, until the veal is browned and the spices are fragrant. Pour in enough water to just cover the veal. Cover the pan and bring to the boil over high heat. Decrease the heat to low–medium, add the parsley, cover and simmer gently for 1½ hours. >

Melt the remaining butter in a separate medium-sized saucepan. Add the onion and garlic, and sauté over low–medium heat for 20 minutes or until golden brown. Add the honey and raisins, and cook, stirring, for a further 5–10 minutes, until sticky like a jam.

Remove the veal from the broth, then cut the meat into smaller chunks and return to the broth. Discard the bones. Add the onion mixture and additional water, if required. Continue to simmer gently for a further 30 minutes.

Pile the couscous onto a large serving plate, making a slight well in the centre. Place the veal in the centre, spoon over the onions and raisins and a little of the broth. Place any remaining broth in a bowl, to be spooned over the couscous as desired.

Medfoun Couscous

Serves 6

1 quantity traditional
  Moroccan couscous (page 54)

120 g (4 oz) butter

500 g (1 lb 2 oz) lamb shoulder
  or leg, cut into small chunks

2 large red onions, coarsely
  chopped

1 clove garlic, finely chopped

1 teaspoon ground cinnamon,
  plus extra to garnish

pinch of saffron threads,
  crumbled

½ teaspoon freshly ground
  black pepper

1 teaspoon salt

icing sugar, to garnish

Prepare the couscous using the traditional method or use instant couscous and follow the directions on the packet.

Heat the butter in the bottom of a large steamer saucepan. Add the lamb, onion, garlic, spices and seasoning, and cook over medium–high heat for 5–10 minutes, until the lamb is browned and the spices are fragrant.

Pour in enough water to just cover the lamb, then cover the pan and bring to the boil. Decrease the heat to low–medium, cover and simmer gently for approximately 2 hours, stirring occasionally, until the stew is thick and the lamb is tender. **>**

Spread half of the couscous onto a large serving plate. Spoon the lamb stew over the top. Cover with the remaining couscous, creating a dome and ensuring the lamb is completely covered. Decorate with cinnamon and icing sugar, creating alternate lines coming down from the top.

Serve with a drink of fresh milk, if desired.

❋ This dish is also known as 'lucky' or 'surprise' couscous because the piled-up couscous conceals the stew underneath.

Couscous with Chicken & Chickpeas

Serves 6

1 quantity traditional
  Moroccan couscous (page 54)

¼ cup (60 ml/2 fl oz) vegetable
  oil

2 tablespoons (40 g/1½ oz)
  butter

1.5-kg (3-lb 5-oz) chicken,
  quartered

2 large red onions, sliced

2 teaspoons ground turmeric

1½ teaspoons paprika

1 teaspoon ground ginger

1 teaspoon ground cinnamon

1 teaspoon ground cumin

½ teaspoon freshly ground
  black pepper

pinch of saffron threads,
  crushed

1 teaspoon salt

½ bunch fresh coriander,
  washed and tied with
  kitchen string

1½ tablespoons tomato paste

1 chicken stock cube

4 medium-sized carrots, cut
  in half across then in half
  lengthways and cored

¼ medium-sized pumpkin,
  coarsely grated

4 medium-sized tomatoes,
  peeled, deseeded and
  coarsely chopped

1 × 300-g (10½-oz) can
  chickpeas, drained and rinsed

Prepare the couscous using the traditional method or use instant couscous
and follow the directions on the packet. >

Heat the oil and butter in the bottom of a large steamer saucepan. Add the chicken, onion, spices and salt, and cook over medium–high heat for 5–10 minutes, until the chicken is browned and the spices are fragrant.

Pour in enough water to just cover the chicken, then add the coriander, tomato paste and crumbled stock cube and bring to the boil. Decrease the heat to low–medium and gently simmer for 30 minutes.

Add the prepared vegetables to the stew and continue to simmer gently for a further 30 minutes. Add the chickpeas and additional water, if required, and continue to simmer gently for a further 20 minutes.

Pile the couscous onto a large serving plate, making a slight well in the centre. Place the chicken pieces in the centre, then spoon on the vegetables and a little of the broth. Place any remaining broth in a bowl, to be spooned over the couscous as desired.

Fish Couscous

Serves 6

1 quantity traditional
Moroccan couscous (page 54)

¼ cup (60 ml/2 fl oz) olive oil

1 large red onion, thickly sliced

2 cloves garlic, finely chopped

2 fresh hot red chillies,
deseeded and finely chopped

1½ teaspoons paprika

1 teaspoon ground cumin

1 teaspoon ground coriander

½ teaspoon freshly ground
black pepper

¼ teaspoon cayenne pepper

1 teaspoon salt

½ bunch fresh coriander,
washed

½ bunch fresh flat-leaf parsley,
washed

4 medium-sized carrots, cut
in half across then in half
lengthways and cored

4 medium-sized tomatoes,
peeled, deseeded and
quartered

1 red capsicum, sliced
lengthways

1 green capsicum, sliced
lengthways

1.25 kg (2 lb 12 oz) snapper or
other firm white fish fillets,
cut into 5-cm (2-in) thick
steaks

Prepare the couscous using the traditional method or use instant couscous
and follow the directions on the packet. >

Heat the oil in the bottom of a large steamer saucepan. Add the onion, garlic, chilli, spices and salt, and cook over low–medium heat for 5–10 minutes, until softened and fragrant.

Tie the coriander and parsley together using kitchen string. Add to the saucepan with the carrot and tomato. Pour in enough water to just cover the vegetables and bring to the boil. Decrease the heat to low–medium and simmer gently for 30 minutes. Add the capsicum to the stew and cook for a further 30 minutes.

Add the fish to the stew and cook for 10–15 minutes, until the fish is cooked and the flesh flakes easily.

Pile the couscous onto a large serving plate, making a slight well in the centre. Place the fish and vegetables in the well and drizzle with a little of the broth. Place any remaining broth in a bowl, to be spooned over the couscous as desired.

Tagines

The tagine is one of Morocco's most well-known dishes and it is very easy to prepare at home. There are many delicious combinations and flavourings. Try the M'qualli Chicken Tagine with Preserved Lemon and Olives (page 94) or a vegetarian dish made with spiced pumpkin and lentils (page 119).

The word 'tagine' applies not only to the meal, but also to the unique cooking vessel in which it is cooked. Tagine cookware is designed especially for slow cooking and has either a domed or conical lid. Steam rises inside to the top of the lid, condenses into liquid and runs down the sides back into the stew cooking below, keeping it moist and creating a flavoursome broth at the same time.

‹ Beef Kefta & Tomato Tagine (page 72)

Beef Kefta & Tomato Tagine

Serves 4

2 tablespoons (40 ml/1½ fl oz) olive oil

1 medium-sized red onion, finely chopped

2 cloves garlic, finely chopped

2 teaspoons sugar

1 teaspoon ground cumin

1 teaspoon paprika

½ teaspoon cayenne pepper

8 medium-sized tomatoes, peeled, deseeded and coarsely chopped

salt and freshly ground black pepper

2 tablespoons finely chopped fresh flat-leaf parsley

BEEF KEFTAS

600 g (1 lb 5 oz) beef mince

1 small red onion, grated

2 tablespoons finely chopped fresh flat-leaf parsley

2 tablespoons finely chopped fresh coriander

1 teaspoon paprika

1 teaspoon ground cumin

½ teaspoon cayenne pepper

¼ teaspoon freshly ground black pepper

½ teaspoon salt

2 tablespoons (40 ml/1½ fl oz) olive oil

Heat the olive oil in a large frying pan over low–medium heat. Add the onion, garlic, sugar and spices, and sauté until golden. Add the tomato and cook for 5 minutes, until softened. Pour in ⅓ cup (80 ml/3 fl oz) water and bring to the boil.

Decrease the heat to low and cook for 10–15 minutes, until the mixture has a sauce-like consistency. Add salt and pepper.

Meanwhile, to make the keftas, combine the mince, onion, parsley, coriander, spices and salt in a bowl. Shape into compact, walnut-sized balls.

Heat the oil in a large frying pan over medium–high heat. Cook the keftas in batches for 3–4 minutes, until browned all over.

Spoon half of the sauce over the base of a medium–large tagine or heavy-based saucepan. Arrange the keftas on top. Spoon on the remaining sauce and sprinkle with the parsley. Cover and cook over low–medium heat for 10–15 minutes, until the keftas are cooked through.

Serve with Moroccan bread (page 225).

Beef & Apple Tagine

Serves 4

¼ cup (60 ml/2 fl oz) olive oil

1 kg (2 lb 3 oz) stewing beef, trimmed and cut into large 5-cm (2-in) chunks

1 large red onion, sliced

1 teaspoon ground ginger

½ teaspoon salt

¼ teaspoon freshly ground black pepper

pinch of saffron threads

1½ cups (375 ml/12½ fl oz) beef stock or water

2 tablespoons (40 g/1½ oz) butter

2 tablespoons honey

3 medium-sized cooking apples, quartered and cored

1 teaspoon ground cinnamon

2 tablespoons finely chopped fresh coriander

Heat the oil in a medium–large tagine or heavy-based saucepan over medium heat. Add the beef, onion, ginger, salt, pepper and saffron, and cook for 5–10 minutes, stirring occasionally, until the beef is browned and the spices are fragrant. Pour in 1¼ cups (310 ml/10½ fl oz) stock or water and bring to the boil. Reduce the heat to low, cover and cook for 1½ hours.

Melt the butter and honey in a medium-sized saucepan over low heat. Add the apple and cinnamon, cover and cook for 10–15 minutes, until almost tender. Arrange apple quarters around the beef in the tagine. Add the remaining stock or water and sprinkle with the coriander. Cover and cook for 30 minutes, or until the meat and apples are tender.

Beef & Sweet Potato Tagine

Serves 4

¼ cup (60 ml/2 fl oz) olive oil

1 kg (2 lb 3 oz) stewing beef, trimmed and cut into 5-cm (2-in) chunks

1 large red onion, sliced into rounds

2 cloves garlic, finely chopped

1 teaspoon paprika

1 teaspoon ground ginger

½ teaspoon cayenne pepper

½ teaspoon ground cumin

¼ teaspoon ground turmeric

¼ teaspoon freshly ground black pepper

½ teaspoon salt

1½ cups (375 ml/12½ fl oz) beef or vegetable stock, or water

1 large sweet potato, sliced into 1-cm (⅜-in) thick rounds

1 tablespoon finely chopped fresh flat-leaf parsley

1 tablespoon finely chopped fresh coriander

Heat the oil in a medium–large tagine or heavy-based saucepan over medium heat. Add the beef, onion, garlic, spices and salt, and cook for 5–10 minutes, stirring occasionally, until the beef is browned and the spices are fragrant. Pour in 1¼ cups (310 ml/10½ fl oz) of the stock or water and bring to the boil. Reduce the heat to low, cover and cook for 1½ hours.

Arrange the sweet potato around the beef and pour in the remaining stock or water. Sprinkle with the parsley and coriander. Cover and cook for a further 30 minutes, until the meat and sweet potato are tender.

Veal & Quince Tagine

Serves 4

¼ cup (60 ml/2 fl oz) olive oil

1.2 kg (2 lb 12 oz) veal osso bucco

1 large red onion, sliced

1½ teaspoons ground ginger

½ teaspoon salt

¼ teaspoon freshly ground black pepper

pinch of saffron threads

1½ cups (375 ml/12½ fl oz) chicken or vegetable stock, or water

2 tablespoons (40 g/1½ oz) butter

2 tablespoons honey

2 quinces, quartered and cored

1 teaspoon ground cinnamon

2 tablespoons finely chopped fresh flat-leaf parsley

Heat the oil in a medium–large tagine or heavy-based saucepan over medium heat. Add the veal, onion, ginger, salt, pepper and saffron, and cook for 5–10 minutes, stirring occasionally, until the veal is browned and the spices are fragrant. Pour in 1¼ cups (310 ml/10½ fl oz) stock or water and bring to the boil. Reduce the heat to low, cover and cook for 1½ hours.

Melt the butter and honey together in a medium saucepan over low heat. Add the quince and cinnamon and cook for 20–30 minutes. Transfer the quince to the tagine, arranging it around the veal. Add the remaining stock or water and sprinkle with the parsley. Cover and cook for a further 30 minutes, until the meat and quince are tender.

Veal, Pea & Artichoke Tagine

Serves 4

¼ cup (60 ml/2 fl oz) olive oil

1.2 kg (2 lb 12 oz) veal osso bucco

2 large red onions, finely chopped

3 cloves garlic, finely chopped

1 teaspoon ground ginger

½ teaspoon ground turmeric

¼ teaspoon freshly ground black pepper

pinch of saffron threads

½ teaspoon salt

1½ cups (375 ml/12½ fl oz) chicken or vegetable stock, or water

8 small artichokes

juice of ½ lemon

1½ cups freshly shelled or frozen peas

2 tablespoons finely chopped fresh coriander

Heat oil in a large tagine or heavy-based saucepan over medium heat. Add veal, onion, garlic, spices and salt, and cook for 5–10 minutes, stirring occasionally, until the veal is browned. Add 1¼ cups (310 ml/10½ fl oz) stock and bring to the boil. Reduce heat to low, cover and cook for 1½ hours.

Discard the artichoke leaves, scoop out the choke and cut off the stalk. Submerge the hearts in a bowl of cold water with the lemon juice added for 10 minutes. Arrange the hearts around the veal. Pour in the remaining stock, cover and cook for a further 20 minutes, until the meat and artichokes are tender. Add the peas and coriander and cook for 10 minutes.

Veal Tagine with Parsley, Preserved Lemon & Olives

Serves 4

¼ cup (60 ml/2 fl oz) olive oil

1.2 kg (2 lb 12 oz) veal osso bucco

2 large red onions, grated

2 cloves garlic, finely chopped

1½ teaspoons ground ginger

1½ teaspoons ground paprika

½ teaspoon ground cinnamon

¼ teaspoon freshly ground black pepper

pinch of saffron threads

½ teaspoon salt

1½ cups (375 ml/12½ fl oz) chicken stock or water

1½ preserved lemons, quartered, flesh discarded and skin thickly sliced

1½ cups finely chopped fresh flat-leaf parsley

⅓ cup green olives

juice of ½ lemon

Heat the oil in a medium–large tagine or heavy-based saucepan over medium heat. Add the veal, onion, garlic, spices and salt, and cook for 5–10 minutes, stirring occasionally, until the veal is browned and the spices are fragrant. Pour in 1¼ cups (310 ml/10½ fl oz) of the stock or water and bring to the boil. Reduce the heat to low, cover and cook for 1½ hours.

Arrange the lemon around the meat. Scatter with the parsley and olives, then pour in the remaining stock or water and the lemon juice. Cover and cook for a further 30 minutes, or until the meat is tender.

Serve with Moroccan bread (page 225).

Veal, Green Bean & Tomato Tagine

Serves 4

¼ cup (60 ml/2 fl oz) olive oil

1.2 kg (2 lb 12 oz) veal osso bucco

1 large onion, sliced

2 cloves garlic, finely chopped

1 tablespoon paprika

1 teaspoon ground ginger

½ teaspoon ground turmeric

¼ teaspoon freshly ground black pepper

pinch of saffron threads

½ teaspoon salt

6 tomatoes, peeled, deseeded and chopped

1½ cups (375 ml/12½ fl oz) chicken or vegetable stock, or water

juice of ½ lemon

450 g (1 lb) green beans, trimmed

Heat the oil in a medium–large tagine or heavy-based saucepan over medium heat. Add the veal, onion, garlic, spices and salt and cook for 5–10 minutes, stirring occasionally, until the veal is browned and the spices are fragrant. Add the tomato, then pour in 1¼ cups (310 ml/10½ fl oz) stock or water and bring to the boil. Reduce heat to low, cover and cook for 1½ hours.

Pour in the remaining stock or water and the lemon juice. Scatter the beans around the outside of the veal. Cover and cook for a further 30 minutes, or until the meat and beans are tender.

Serve with Moroccan bread (page 225).

Veal & Cauliflower Tagine

Serves 4

¼ cup (60 ml/2 fl oz) olive oil

1.2 kg (2 lb 12 oz) veal osso bucco

1 large onion, finely chopped

2 cloves garlic, finely chopped

1½ teaspoons ground cumin

1 teaspoon ground ginger

½ teaspoon ground turmeric

¼ teaspoon freshly ground black pepper

pinch of saffron threads

½ teaspoon salt

1½ cups (375 ml/12½ fl oz) chicken stock or water

1 cauliflower, cut into florets

juice of ½ lemon

2 tomatoes, peeled, deseeded and coarsely chopped

2 tablespoons finely chopped fresh coriander

Heat the oil in a medium–large tagine or heavy-based saucepan over medium heat. Add the veal, onion, garlic, spices and salt, and cook for 5–10 minutes, stirring occasionally, until the veal is browned and the spices are fragrant. Pour in 1¼ cups (310 ml/10½ fl oz) stock or water and bring to the boil. Reduce the heat to low, cover and cook for 1¼ hours.

Arrange cauliflower around the veal. Pour in remaining stock or water and lemon juice. Scatter tomato in the centre and sprinkle with coriander. Cover and cook for 30–45 minutes, until the meat and cauliflower are tender.

Serve with Moroccan bread (page 225).

Lamb & Prune Tagine

Serves 4

¼ cup (60 ml/2 fl oz) olive oil

1-kg (2-lb 3-oz) boneless lamb shoulder or leg, trimmed and cut in 5-cm (2-in) chunks

2 large red onions, sliced

1½ teaspoons ground cinnamon

1½ teaspoons ground ginger

1 teaspoon ground cumin

¼ teaspoon freshly ground black pepper

pinch of saffron threads

½ teaspoon salt

1½ cups (375 ml/12½ fl oz) chicken or vegetable stock, or water

1½ cups pitted prunes

2 teaspoons sesame seeds, toasted

Heat the oil in a medium–large tagine or heavy-based saucepan over medium heat. Add the lamb, onion, spices and salt, and cook for 5–10 minutes, stirring occasionally, until the lamb is browned and the spices fragrant. Pour in 1¼ cups (310 ml/10½ fl oz) of the stock or water and bring to the boil. Reduce the heat to low, cover and cook for 1½ hours.

Pour in the remaining stock or water and scatter with the prunes. Cover and cook for a further 30 minutes, until the meat is tender. Sprinkle with the sesame seeds.

Serve with Moroccan bread (page 225).

Lamb & Fennel Tagine

Serves 4

¼ cup (60 ml/2 fl oz) olive oil

1.2 kg (2 lb 12 oz) lamb chump chops

1 large red onion, sliced

2 cloves garlic, finely chopped

1½ teaspoons ground ginger

½ teaspoon ground turmeric

¼ teaspoon freshly ground black pepper

pinch of saffron threads

½ teaspoon salt

1½ cups (375 ml/12½ fl oz) chicken or vegetable stock, or water

3 bulbs baby fennel

juice of ½ lemon

1 tablespoon finely chopped fresh flat-leaf parsley

1 tablespoon finely chopped fresh coriander

Heat the oil in a medium–large tagine or heavy-based saucepan over medium heat. Add the lamb, onion, garlic, spices and salt, and cook for 5–10 minutes, stirring occasionally, until the lamb is browned and the spices are fragrant. Pour in 1¼ cups (310 ml/10½ fl oz) stock or water and bring to the boil. Reduce the heat to low, cover and cook for 1¼ hours.

Remove and discard the tough outer layers from the fennel and cut the bulbs into quarters. Arrange the fennel pieces around the lamb, pour the lemon juice over and sprinkle with the parsley and coriander. Pour in the remaining stock or water, cover and cook for a further 30–45 minutes, until the meat and fennel are tender. Serve with Moroccan bread (page 225).

Lamb Tagine with Raisins & Almonds

Serves 4

2 tablespoons (40 ml/1½ fl oz) olive oil

2 tablespoons (40 g/1½ oz) butter

4 × 300–350-g (10½–12-oz) lamb shanks

2 large red onions, grated

1½ teaspoons ground cinnamon

1½ teaspoons ground ginger

pinch of saffron threads

¼ teaspoon black pepper

½ teaspoon salt

1½ cups (375 ml/12½ fl oz) chicken or vegetable stock, or water

1 cup raisins

¼ cup (60 ml/2 fl oz) vegetable oil

½ cup blanched almonds

Heat the olive oil and butter in a medium–large tagine or heavy-based saucepan over medium heat. Add the lamb, onion, spices and salt, and cook for 5–10 minutes, stirring occasionally, until the lamb is browned and the spices are fragrant. Pour in 1¼ cups (310 ml/10½ fl oz) of the stock or water and bring to the boil. Reduce the heat to low, cover and cook for 1½ hours.

Pour in the remaining stock or water and scatter with the raisins. Cover and cook for a further 30 minutes, or until the meat is tender.

Meanwhile, heat the vegetable oil in a small frying pan over low–medium heat. Add the almonds and cook for 2–3 minutes, until golden brown. Scatter the tagine with the almonds and serve with Moroccan bread (page 225).

Lamb Tagine with Tomato & Green Capsicum

Serves 4

2 green capsicums

¼ cup (60 ml/2 fl oz) olive oil

1.2 kg (2 lb 12 oz) lamb chump chops

1 large red onion, finely chopped

2 cloves garlic, finely chopped

1 tablespoon paprika

1 teaspoon ground ginger

1 teaspoon ground cumin

¼ teaspoon freshly ground black pepper

¼ teaspoon cayenne pepper

pinch of saffron threads

½ teaspoon salt

6 tomatoes, peeled, deseeded and chopped

1½ cups (375 ml/12½ fl oz) chicken or vegetable stock, or water

juice of ½ lemon

1 tablespoon finely chopped fresh flat-leaf parsley

Preheat the oven to 240°C (460°F).

Roast the capsicums until the skins blister and blacken (about 15 minutes). Place in a bowl, cover with cling wrap and set aside to sweat and cool slightly. Peel the capsicums and discard the seeds. Slice the flesh into thick lengths and set aside. **>**

Heat the oil in a medium–large tagine or heavy-based saucepan over medium heat. Add the lamb, onion, garlic, spices and salt, and cook for 5–10 minutes, stirring occasionally, until the lamb is browned and the spices are fragrant. Add the tomato, then pour in 1¼ cups (310 ml/ 10½ fl oz) of the stock or water and bring to the boil. Reduce the heat to low, cover and cook for 1½ hours.

Pour in the remaining stock or water and the lemon juice. Arrange the capsicum around the outside of the lamb and scatter with the parsley. Cover and cook for a further 30 minutes, or until the meat is tender.

Serve with Moroccan bread (page 225).

Chicken, Prune & Almond Tagine

Serves 4

2 tablespoons (40 ml/1½ fl oz) olive oil

1 tablespoon (20 g/¾ oz) butter

1 × 1.6-kg (3 lb 8-oz) chicken, cut into 8 pieces

2 large red onions, grated

1½ teaspoons ground cinnamon

1 teaspoon ground ginger

¼ teaspoon freshly ground black pepper

pinch of saffron threads

½ teaspoon salt

1¼ cups (310 ml/10½ fl oz) chicken or vegetable stock, or water

1 tablespoon honey

1½ cups pitted prunes

¼ cup (60 ml/2 fl oz) vegetable oil

½ cup whole blanched almonds

Heat the olive oil and butter in a large tagine or heavy-based saucepan over medium heat. Add the chicken, onion, spices and salt, and cook for 5–10 minutes, stirring occasionally, until the chicken is browned and the spices are fragrant. Pour in the honey and 1 cup (250 ml/8½ fl oz) stock or water and bring to the boil. Reduce the heat to low, cover and cook for 20 minutes. Scatter with prunes, then pour in the remaining stock or water, cover and cook for 20–30 minutes, until the chicken is cooked.

Meanwhile, heat the vegetable oil in a small frying pan over low–medium heat. Add the almonds and cook for 2–3 minutes, until golden brown. Sprinkle the almonds over the tagine and serve with Moroccan bread (page 225).

M'qualli Chicken Tagine with Preserved Lemon & Olives

Serves 4

¼ cup (60 ml/2 fl oz) olive oil

1 × 1.6-kg (3 lb 8-oz) chicken, cut into 8 pieces

1 large red onion, sliced

2 cloves garlic, finely chopped

1½ teaspoons ground ginger

1 teaspoon ground cumin

¼ teaspoon freshly ground black pepper

pinch of saffron threads

½ teaspoon salt

1¼ cups (310 ml/10½ fl oz) chicken or vegetable stock, or water

2 preserved lemons, quartered, flesh discarded and skin sliced

½ cup green olives

2 tablespoons finely chopped fresh flat-leaf parsley

2 tablespoons finely chopped fresh coriander

Heat the oil in a medium–large tagine or heavy-based saucepan over medium heat. Add the chicken, onion, garlic, spices and salt, and cook for 5–10 minutes, stirring occasionally, until the chicken is browned and the spices are fragrant. Pour in 1 cup (250 ml/8½ fl oz) stock or water and bring to the boil. Reduce the heat to low, cover and cook for 20 minutes.

Arrange the preserved lemon around the chicken and scatter with the olives. Sprinkle with the parsley and coriander. Pour in the remaining stock or water, cover and cook for 25–30 minutes, until the chicken is cooked.

Serve with Moroccan bread (page 225).

Chicken & Apricot Tagine

Serves 4

¼ cup (60 ml/2 fl oz) olive oil

1 × 1.6-kg (3 lb 8-oz) chicken,
  cut into 8 pieces

1 large red onion, sliced

1 teaspoon ground cinnamon

1 teaspoon ground ginger

¼ teaspoon freshly ground
  black pepper

pinch of saffron threads

½ teaspoon salt

1¼ cups (310 ml/10½ fl oz)
  chicken or vegetable stock,
  or water

1 tablespoon honey

1½ cups dried apricots

2 tablespoons finely chopped
  fresh coriander

Heat the oil in a medium–large tagine or heavy-based saucepan over medium heat. Add the chicken, onion, spices and salt, and cook for 5–10 minutes, stirring occasionally, until the chicken is browned and the spices are fragrant. Pour in 1 cup (250 ml/8½ fl oz) of the stock or water and the honey, and bring to the boil. Reduce the heat to low, cover and cook for 20 minutes.

Scatter the chicken with apricots and coriander. Pour in the remaining stock or water, then cover and cook for a further 25–30 minutes, until the chicken is cooked.

Serve with Moroccan bread (page 225).

Chicken Tagine
with Pumpkin Jam

Serves 4

1 × 1.6-kg (3 lb 8-oz) chicken, cut into 8 pieces

½ small bunch fresh coriander, washed and tied with kitchen string

6 cloves garlic, finely chopped

2 tablespoons (40 ml/1½ fl oz) olive oil

2 tablespoons (40 g/1½ oz) butter

1½ teaspoons ground ginger

1 teaspoon ground cumin

¼ teaspoon freshly ground black pepper

½ teaspoon salt

2 preserved lemons, deseeded and coarsely chopped

⅓ cup (80 ml/3 fl oz) chicken or vegetable stock, or water

2 medium-sized red onions, quartered

½ cup green olives

PUMPKIN JAM

1 kg (2 lb 3 oz) pumpkin, very finely sliced

1 tablespoon (20 ml/¾ fl oz) vegetable oil

pinch of salt

3 tablespoons honey

1 tablespoon (15 g/½ oz) sugar

½ teaspoon ground cinnamon

To make the jam, place the pumpkin, oil and salt in a large non-stick frying pan over low heat. Cover and cook, stirring occasionally, for 20–25 minutes or until the pumpkin is soft. Add the honey, sugar and cinnamon and mash together. Cook, uncovered, for a further 45–60 minutes, until the pumpkin is thick, sticky and dark orange. Keep warm. >

Meanwhile, place the chicken, coriander, garlic, oil, butter, spices, salt, half the lemon and half the stock or water in a medium–large tagine or heavy-based saucepan over low–medium heat. Reduce the heat to low, cover and cook for 20 minutes. Add the onion and cook for a further 25–30 minutes, until the chicken is cooked.

Remove the chicken, set aside on a plate and cover to keep warm. Remove and discard the coriander.

Mash the onion mixture and liquid together and cook, uncovered, for 10 minutes or until the sauce has thickened. Add the remaining lemon and the olives and stir to combine.

When you are almost ready to serve the tagine, return the chicken to the pot and heat through, coating it in the sauce.

Serve with the pumpkin jam and Moroccan bread (page 225).

Fish & Olive Tagine

Serves 4

¼ cup (60 ml/2 fl oz) olive oil

2 cloves garlic, finely chopped

1 teaspoon ground ginger

½ teaspoon ground turmeric

pinch of saffron threads

¼ teaspoon freshly ground
black pepper

½ teaspoon salt

4 × 200-g (7-oz) snapper
cutlets, or other firm white
fish pieces

1 large carrot, sliced into
1-cm (⅜-in) thick rounds

1 large red onion, sliced into
thick rounds

2 tomatoes, sliced into
thick rounds

1 lemon, sliced into rounds

½ cup green olives

2 tablespoons finely chopped
fresh coriander

Combine the oil, garlic, spices and salt in a large bowl. Add the fish and toss to coat. Cover and place in the refrigerator to marinate for at least 6 hours or overnight.

Arrange the carrot in the base of a medium–large tagine or flameproof dish. Cover with half the onion, followed by the marinated fish and then the remaining onion. Arrange the tomato and lemon around the fish and scatter with the olives. Pour in ⅓ cup (80 ml/3 fl oz) water and any remaining marinade and sprinkle with the coriander. Cover and cook over medium heat for 25–30 minutes, until the fish is cooked.

Fish & Saffron Tagine

Serves 4

2 tablespoons (40 ml/1½ fl oz)
olive oil

2 tablespoons (40 g/1½ oz)
butter

2 large onions, sliced

1 teaspoon ground ginger

¼ teaspoon freshly ground
black pepper

2 pinches saffron threads

½ teaspoon salt

1 large carrot, cut into 1-cm
(⅜-in) thick rounds

800 g (2 lb 12 oz) snapper, or
other firm white fish, cut
into 10-cm (4-in) pieces

1 preserved lemon, quartered,
flesh discarded and skin
sliced

Heat the oil and butter in a medium-sized frying pan over low–medium heat. Add the onion, spices and salt, and sauté until softened and fragrant.

Arrange the carrot in the base of a medium–large tagine or flameproof dish. Layer half of the spiced onion mixture on top, followed by the fish and then the remaining onion. Arrange the lemon quarters around the fish. Pour in ⅓ cup (80 ml/3 fl oz) water. Cover and cook over medium heat for 25–30 minutes, until the fish is cooked.

Serve with Moroccan bread (page 225).

Fish-ball Tagine

Serves 4

1 kg (2 lb 3 oz) hapuka
fillets, or other firm white
fish fillets, skin and bones
removed

2 tablespoons fine soft
breadcrumbs

1 small carrot, cut into rounds

1 tablespoon finely chopped
fresh coriander

CHERMOULA PASTE

2 cloves garlic, chopped

2 tablespoons finely chopped
fresh coriander leaves

2 tablespoons finely chopped
fresh flat-leaf parsley leaves

1 tablespoon (20 ml/¾ fl oz)
olive oil

1 tablespoon (20 ml/¾ fl oz)
lemon juice

1 teaspoon paprika

1 teaspoon ground cumin

1 teaspoon ground coriander

¼ teaspoon ground black pepper

½ teaspoon salt

TOMATO SAUCE

2 tablespoons (40 ml/1½ fl oz)
olive oil

1 onion, finely chopped

2 teaspoons sugar

1 teaspoon ground cumin

1 teaspoon paprika

½ teaspoon ground turmeric

8 tomatoes, peeled, deseeded
and coarsely chopped

salt and ground black pepper

To make the chermoula paste, place the garlic, coriander and parsley in a
food processor and blend to a paste. Add the oil, lemon juice, spices and
salt and blend to combine. >

Coarsely chop the fish fillets and pass through a mouli or mincer, or finely chop in a food processor. Combine the fish mince, chermoula paste and breadcrumbs in a medium-sized bowl. Shape into walnut-sized balls, cover and refrigerate until required.

To make the tomato sauce, heat the oil in a large frying pan over low–medium heat. Add the onion, sugar and spices, and sauté until softened and fragrant. Add the tomato and cook for 5 minutes, until softened. Pour in ⅓ cup (80 ml/3 fl oz) water and bring to the boil. Season with salt and pepper.

Spoon half the tomato sauce into the base of a medium–large tagine or flameproof dish and arrange the fish balls on top. Cover with the remaining sauce and sprinkle with the coriander. Cover and cook over low–medium heat for 15–20 minutes, until the fish is cooked.

Serve with Moroccan bread (page 225).

Fish, Date & Onion Tagine

Serves 4

2 tablespoons (40 ml/1½ fl oz) olive oil

2 tablespoons (40 g/1½ oz) butter

1 tablespoon honey

2 large red onions, cut into rounds

1 teaspoon ground ginger

1 teaspoon ground cinnamon

¼ teaspoon freshly ground black pepper

pinch of saffron threads

½ teaspoon salt

1½ cups pitted dried dates

1 large carrot, cut into 1-cm (⅜-in) thick rounds

4 × 200-g (7-oz) snapper cutlets, or other firm white fish

¼ cup (60 ml/2 fl oz) vegetable oil

¼ cup whole blanched almonds

Heat the olive oil, butter and honey in a frying pan over low–medium heat. Add the onion, spices and salt, and sauté until softened. Stir in the dates.

Arrange the carrot in the base of a medium–large tagine. Layer half the onion mixture on top, followed by the fish and the remaining onion. Pour in ⅓ cup (80 ml/3 fl oz) water, cover and cook over medium heat for 25–30 minutes.

Meanwhile, heat the vegetable oil in a small frying pan over low–medium heat. Add the almonds and cook for 2–3 minutes, until golden brown. Scatter the tagine with almonds and serve with Moroccan bread (page 225).

Fish, Tomato & Zucchini Tagine

Serves 4

2 tablespoons (40 ml/1½ fl oz) olive oil

1 large red onion, finely chopped

1 teaspoon ground coriander

1 teaspoon ground cumin

½ teaspoon ground turmeric

¼ teaspoon freshly ground black pepper

pinch of saffron threads

½ teaspoon salt

4 tomatoes, peeled, deseeded and coarsely chopped

1 preserved lemon, flesh discarded and skin coarsely chopped

1 large carrot, cut into 1-cm (⅜-in) thick rounds

4 × 180-g (6½-oz) thick swordfish steaks

2 medium-sized zucchini, quartered lengthways and deseeded

2 tablespoons finely chopped fresh coriander

Heat the oil in a medium-sized frying pan over low–medium heat. Add the onion, spices and salt, and sauté until softened and fragrant.

Add the tomato to the pan and cook for 5 minutes, until softened. Pour in ⅓ cup (80 ml/3 fl oz) water and bring to the boil. Decrease the heat to low, add the preserved lemon and stir to combine.

Arrange the carrot in the base of a medium–large tagine or flameproof dish. Spoon half the sauce over and lay the fish on top. Arrange the zucchini around the fish and cover the fish and zucchini with the remaining sauce. Sprinkle with the coriander, cover and cook over medium heat for 25–30 minutes, until the fish is cooked.

Serve with Moroccan bread (page 225).

Spicy Tuna, Potato & Green Capsicum Tagine

Serves 4

4 × 180-g (6½-oz) thick tuna steaks

1 large carrot, sliced into 1-cm (⅜-in) thick rounds

1 large red onion, sliced into rounds

2 medium-sized potatoes, thickly sliced lengthways

2 green capsicums, sliced into 1-cm (⅜-in) thick rings

1 lemon, sliced into rounds

CHERMOULA PASTE

3 cloves garlic, chopped

½ bunch fresh coriander, leaves chopped

½ bunch fresh flat-leaf parsley, leaves chopped

¼ cup (60 ml/2 fl oz) olive oil

¼ cup (60 ml/2 fl oz) lemon juice

1½ teaspoons paprika

1 teaspoon ground cumin

1 teaspoon ground coriander

½ teaspoon freshly ground black pepper

½ teaspoon salt

To make the chermoula paste, place the garlic, coriander and parsley in a food processor and blend to a paste. Add the oil, lemon juice, spices and salt, and blend to combine.

Combine the fish and chermoula paste in a large bowl and toss to coat. Cover and place in the refrigerator to marinate for at least 6 hours or overnight. **>**

Arrange the carrot in the base of a medium–large tagine or flameproof dish. Layer the onion on top, followed by the marinated fish. Arrange the potato and capsicum slices around the fish. Top with the lemon slices and pour in ⅓ cup (80 ml/3 fl oz) water and any remaining marinade. Cover and cook over medium heat for 25–30 minutes, until the fish is cooked.

Serve with Moroccan bread (page 225).

Vegetable Tagine

Serves 4

¼ cup (60 ml/2 fl oz) olive oil

1 large red onion, sliced

2 cloves garlic, finely chopped

1 teaspoon paprika

1 teaspoon ground ginger

1 teaspoon ground cumin

½ teaspoon ground turmeric

½ teaspoon cayenne pepper

¼ teaspoon freshly ground black pepper

pinch of saffron threads

½ teaspoon salt

2 medium-sized carrots, quartered lengthways and cored

1 sweet potato, sliced into rounds

2 medium-sized potatoes, thickly sliced lengthways

2 medium-sized zucchini, quartered lengthways and deseeded

2 tomatoes, peeled, deseeded and coarsely chopped

1 green capsicum, thickly sliced lengthways

½ cup fresh or frozen peas

2 tablespoons finely chopped fresh flat-leaf parsley

2 tablespoons finely chopped fresh coriander

⅓ cup (80 ml/3 fl oz) vegetable stock or water

Heat the oil in a medium–large tagine or heavy-based saucepan over medium heat. Add the onion, garlic, spices and salt, and sauté until softened and fragrant. ❯

Arrange the vegetables in the tagine in layers, starting with the carrot, then the sweet potato, potato, zucchini, tomato and capsicum. Scatter with the peas and sprinkle with the parsley and coriander.

Pour in the stock or water and bring to the boil. Reduce the heat to low, cover and cook for 20–30 minutes, or until the vegetables are tender.

Serve with Moroccan bread (page 225).

Pumpkin & Sweet Potato Tagine

Serves 4

¼ cup (60 ml/2 fl oz) olive oil

2 medium-sized red onions, sliced

3 cloves garlic, finely chopped

1 teaspoon ground ginger

1 teaspoon ground cinnamon

½ teaspoon ground turmeric

½ teaspoon cayenne pepper

¼ teaspoon freshly ground black pepper

pinch of saffron threads

½ teaspoon salt

450 g (1 lb) pumpkin, cut into 4-cm (1½-in) cubes

450 g (1 lb) sweet potato, cut into 4-cm (1½-in) cubes

¾ cup (180 ml/6 fl oz) vegetable stock or water

¼ cup (60 ml/2 fl oz) vegetable oil

½ cup whole blanched almonds

Heat the olive oil in a medium–large tagine or heavy-based saucepan over medium heat. Add the onion, garlic, spices and salt, and sauté until softened and fragrant. Add the pumpkin and sweet potato and cook, stirring, for 5–10 minutes or until golden brown. Pour in the stock or water and bring to the boil. Decrease the heat to low, cover and cook for 20–30 minutes, until the pumpkin and sweet potato are tender.

Meanwhile, heat the vegetable oil in a small frying pan over low–medium heat. Add the almonds and cook for 2–3 minutes, until golden brown. Drain on paper towel. Sprinkle the almonds over the tagine and serve.

Zucchini, Tomato & Chickpea Tagine

Serves 4

1 cup dried chickpeas

¼ cup (60 ml/2 fl oz) olive oil

1 large red onion, sliced

2 cloves garlic, finely chopped

1 teaspoon paprika

1 teaspoon ground cumin

½ teaspoon ground ginger

½ teaspoon ground turmeric

½ teaspoon cayenne pepper

¼ teaspoon freshly ground black pepper

½ teaspoon salt

4 medium-sized tomatoes, peeled and quartered

2 medium-sized zucchini, quartered and deseeded

2 tablespoons finely chopped fresh flat-leaf parsley

2 tablespoons finely chopped fresh coriander

⅓ cup (80 ml/3 fl oz) vegetable stock or water

Soak the chickpeas in cold water for at least 6 hours or overnight. Drain and rinse the chickpeas and place in a medium-sized saucepan. Cover with cold water and bring to the boil over high heat. Cook for 1 hour, until tender. Drain and set aside.

Heat the oil in a medium–large tagine or heavy-based saucepan over medium heat. Add the onion, garlic, spices and salt, and sauté until softened and fragrant. Add the chickpeas, tomato, zucchini, parsley and coriander and stir to combine. Pour in the stock or water and bring to the boil. Reduce the heat to low, cover and cook for 20–30 minutes, until the vegetables are tender.

Spicy Pumpkin & Lentil Tagine

Serves 4–6

½ cup dried green lentils

1 L (34 fl oz) vegetable stock
or water

¼ cup (60 ml/2 fl oz) olive oil

1 large brown onion, sliced

3 cloves garlic, finely chopped

2 teaspoons paprika

1 teaspoon ground turmeric

1 teaspoon ground cumin

½ teaspoon cayenne pepper

¼ teaspoon black pepper

½ teaspoon salt

2 tomatoes, peeled, deseeded
and coarsely chopped

3 teaspoons tomato paste

700 g (1 lb 9 oz) pumpkin, cut
into 4-cm (1½-in) cubes

¼ cup raisins

2 tablespoons chopped fresh
flat-leaf parsley

2 tablespoons chopped fresh
coriander

Place the lentils and stock or water in a medium-sized saucepan over medium–high heat and bring to the boil. Decrease the heat to low, cover and cook for 15–20 minutes, until the lentils are just tender. Set aside.

Heat the oil in a medium–large tagine or heavy-based saucepan over medium heat. Add the onion, garlic, spices and salt, and sauté until softened and fragrant. Add the tomato and tomato paste, and stir to combine. Add the pumpkin and (undrained) lentils. Scatter with the raisins and bring to the boil. Decrease the heat to low, cover and cook for 20–30 minutes, until the pumpkin is tender. Sprinkle with the parsley and coriander.

Seafood

Seafood is found in abundance in the Moroccan towns and villages that line the Atlantic coast. Fish and seafood fresh off the boat are sold at markets daily.

You can even take fish from the market straight to a nearby food stall where it will be cooked over hot coals, then seasoned simply with rock salt and a drizzle of oil.

‹ Grilled Sardines (page 122)

Grilled Sardines

Serves 4

2 large red onions, sliced into rounds

2 kg (4 lb 6 oz) whole fresh sardines, scaled and gutted

drizzle of olive oil

salt and freshly ground black pepper

2 lemons, cut into wedges

HARISSA-SPICED TOMATO SAUCE

1 tablespoon (20 ml/¾ fl oz) olive oil

4 medium-sized tomatoes, peeled, deseeded and finely chopped

2 tablespoons harissa paste (page 233)

1 tablespoon (20 ml/¾ fl oz) lemon juice

½ cup finely chopped fresh coriander

salt and freshly ground black pepper

To make the harissa-spiced tomato sauce, heat the oil in a large frying pan over low–medium heat. Add the tomato and sauté for 5 minutes, until softened. Add the harissa paste, lemon juice and coriander, stir to combine, and cook for a further 2 minutes. Season with salt and pepper. Cover and refrigerate until required.

Preheat barbecue to medium–high.

Spread one-quarter of the onions on a flat wire barbecue grill tray that can be closed and secured. Lay half of the sardines on top and cover with another quarter of the onions. Close and secure the grill tray. Drizzle with oil and sprinkle with salt and pepper on both sides. Cook the sardines for 5 minutes on each side, until cooked through.

Repeat the process with the remaining sardines and onion.

Serve with the lemon wedges and harissa-spiced tomato sauce.

Trout Filled with Stuffed Dates

Serves 4

2 × 1-kg (2 lb 3-oz) whole trout, scaled and cleaned

drizzle of olive oil

salt and freshly ground black pepper

¼ cup flaked almonds

STUFFED DATES

¼ cup long-grain rice, rinsed

100 g (3½ oz) butter

1 medium-sized red onion, finely chopped

1 teaspoon ground cinnamon

1 teaspoon ground ginger

¾ cup (75 g/2½ oz) ground almonds

500 g fresh dates, pitted

Preheat the oven to 180°C (360°F).

To make the stuffed dates, bring a small saucepan of water to the boil. Add the rice and cook for 3 minutes. Drain and set aside to cool.

Melt 2 tablespoons (40 g/1½ oz) of the butter in a small frying pan over low–medium heat. Add the onion and spices, and sauté until the onion is soft and the spices are fragrant.

Combine the cooled rice, spiced onion and ground almonds in a medium-sized bowl, mixing well. Stuff the dates with the rice filling and place inside the fish cavities, along with any remaining filling. Secure the edges of the cavities using toothpicks.

Lay each fish on a sheet of aluminium foil large enough to encase it. Drizzle with oil and season with salt and pepper. Dot with the remaining butter and sprinkle with the flaked almonds. Wrap the foil around each fish to enclose completely.

Bake in the oven for 15–25 minutes, until cooked through and the flesh flakes easily. Remove the toothpicks and serve.

Grilled Chermoula Fish

Serves 4

1 × 1.5-kg (3 lb 5-oz) whole snapper, scaled and cleaned

3 medium-sized tomatoes, sliced into rounds

1 large red onion, sliced into rounds

2 lemons, cut into wedges

CHERMOULA PASTE

3 cloves garlic, chopped

½ bunch fresh coriander, leaves chopped

½ bunch fresh flat-leaf parsley, leaves chopped

¼ cup (60 ml/2 fl oz) olive oil

¼ cup (60 ml/2 fl oz) lemon juice

1½ teaspoons paprika

1 teaspoon ground cumin

1 teaspoon ground coriander

½ teaspoon freshly ground black pepper

½ teaspoon salt

To make the chermoula paste, place the garlic, coriander and parsley in a food processor and blend to a paste. Add the oil, lemon juice, spices and salt and blend to combine.

Score the fish twice in the thickest part near the head to ensure even cooking. Place the fish in a large dish and coat with chermoula, filling the cavity and scored cuts. Cover and place in the refrigerator to marinate for at least 6 hours or overnight.

Preheat the oven to 200°C (390°F). ❯

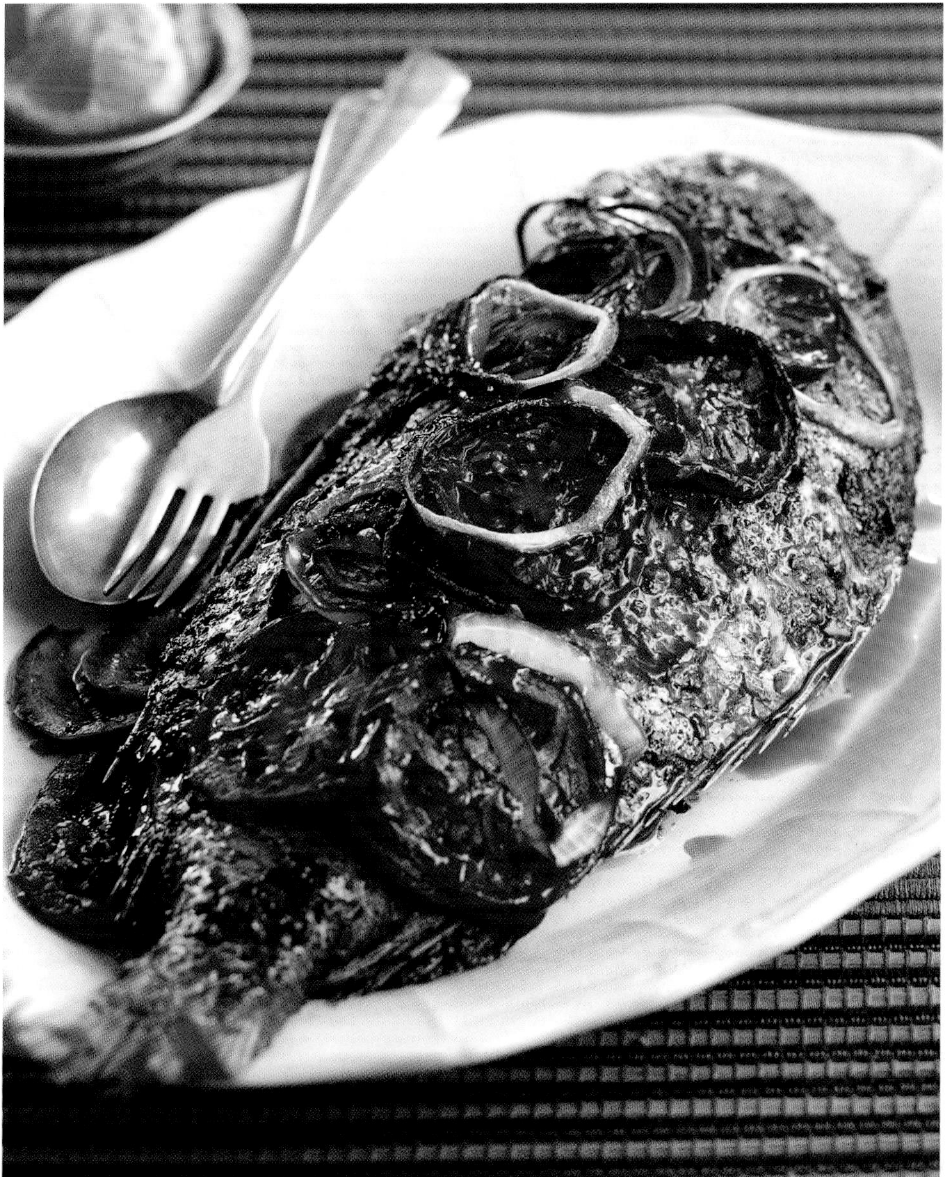

Lay half the tomato and onion slices in the base of a large baking dish. Place the marinated fish on top and cover with the remaining tomato and onion. Bake in the oven for 25–30 minutes, until cooked through and the flesh flakes easily.

Serve with lemon wedges.

Fish with Preserved Lemon & Olives

Serves 4

1 × 1.5-kg (3 lb 5-oz) whole
   bream, scaled and cleaned

¼ cup (60 ml/2 fl oz) olive oil

¼ cup (60 ml/2 fl oz) lemon juice

1 clove garlic, crushed

1½ teaspoons ground ginger

1 teaspoon ground cumin

½ teaspoon ground turmeric

¼ teaspoon freshly ground
   black pepper

½ teaspoon salt

2 preserved lemons, quartered,
   flesh discarded and skin
   finely sliced

1 small red onion, sliced

¼ cup green olives

Score the fish twice in the thickest part near the head to ensure even cooking, and place in a large dish.

Combine the oil, lemon juice, garlic, spices and salt in a medium-sized bowl. Add the lemon and onion. Pour the mixture over the fish, rubbing to coat and filling the cavity and scored cuts. Cover and place in the refrigerator to marinate for at least 6 hours or overnight.

Preheat the oven to 200°C (390°F).

Lay the marinated fish on a sheet of aluminium foil large enough to encase it. Scatter with the olives, drizzle with any remaining marinade and wrap the foil around the fish, folding the edges to seal. Bake for 25–30 minutes, until cooked through and the flesh flakes easily.

Fried Fish with Chermoula Paste

Serves 4

1 cup (150 g/5 oz) semolina
flour

1 teaspoon ground cumin

1 teaspoon ground ginger

½ teaspoon freshly ground
black pepper

1 teaspoon salt

2 large eggs

900 g (2 lb) flathead tails

vegetable oil, for deep-frying

2 lemons, cut into wedges

CHERMOULA PASTE

3 cloves garlic, chopped

½ bunch fresh coriander,
leaves chopped

½ bunch fresh flat-leaf parsley,
leaves chopped

¼ cup (60 ml/2 fl oz) olive oil

¼ cup (60 ml/2 fl oz) lemon
juice

1½ teaspoons paprika

1 teaspoon ground cumin

1 teaspoon ground coriander

½ teaspoon freshly ground
black pepper

½ teaspoon salt

To make the chermoula paste, place the garlic, coriander and parsley in a food processor and blend to a paste. Add the olive oil, lemon juice, spices and salt and blend to combine.

To prepare the fish, combine the semolina flour, spices and salt in a medium-sized bowl. Lightly beat the eggs in a separate bowl. Coat the flathead tails by dipping each one in the beaten egg followed by the spiced flour.

Preheat vegetable oil in a large, heavy-based frying pan suitable for deep-frying. Fry the fish in batches for 1–2 minutes on each side, or until cooked through. Drain on paper towel and keep warm until all the fish are cooked.

Serve with lemon wedges and chermoula paste for dipping.

Harissa Prawns

Serves 4

1.2 kg (2 lb 12 oz) raw (green) tiger prawns, shelled and deveined

salt and freshly ground black pepper

2 lemons, cut into wedges

HARISSA MARINADE

¼ cup (60 ml/2 fl oz) olive oil

2 tablespoons (40 ml/1½ fl oz) lemon juice

2 tablespoons (20 g/¾ oz) ground almonds

1 tablespoon finely chopped fresh flat-leaf parsley

1 tablespoon finely chopped fresh coriander

1 clove garlic, crushed

2 teaspoons harissa paste (page 233)

1 teaspoon paprika

½ teaspoon ground cumin

½ teaspoon ground ginger

½ teaspoon ground turmeric

Combine all the marinade ingredients in a medium-sized bowl. Add the prawns and toss to coat. Season with salt and pepper. Cover and place in the refrigerator to marinate for at least 6 hours or overnight.

Preheat a large non-stick frying pan over high heat. Cook the prawns with the marinade for 1–2 minutes on each side, or until they turn pink and begin to firm up.

Serve with the lemon wedges.

Stewed Octopus

Serves 4

1 × 1.25-kg (2 lb 12-oz)
octopus

2 tablespoons (40 ml/1½ fl oz)
olive oil

1 large red onion, finely
chopped

1 clove garlic, finely chopped

1 bay leaf

1 teaspoon paprika

½ teaspoon ground cumin

¼ teaspoon cayenne pepper

4 medium-sized tomatoes,
peeled, deseeded and
coarsely chopped

juice of 1 lemon

½ cup finely chopped fresh
coriander

salt and freshly ground black
pepper

steamed or boiled long-grain
rice, to serve

Wash the octopus under cold running water and remove the guts and the ink sac. Place the octopus in a large saucepan, cover with cold water and bring to the boil. Decrease the heat to medium and simmer for 1 hour. Drain and set the octopus aside to cool slightly.

Peel the thin outer membrane off the octopus. Remove and discard the head, cutting away the beak. Cut the remaining flesh and tentacles into 2-cm (¾-in) thick pieces.

Heat the oil in a medium-sized saucepan over low–medium heat. Add the onion, garlic, bay leaf and spices, and sauté until softened and fragrant. Add the octopus, tomato and lemon juice, and cook over low heat for 20–25 minutes, until the sauce is thick and the octopus tender. Add the coriander and season with salt and pepper.

To serve, pile the rice onto a large serving plate and spoon the octopus and sauce over the top.

Seafood Bastilla

Serves 6–8

200 g (7 oz) vermicelli rice
  noodles

1 cup (250 ml/8½ fl oz) fish
  stock

juice of 1 lemon

1 kg (2 lb 3 oz) rockling fillets

¼ cup (60 ml/2 fl oz) olive oil

1 large red onion, finely
  chopped

1 teaspoon ground ginger

1 teaspoon ground turmeric

1 teaspoon ground cumin

½ teaspoon cayenne pepper

pinch of saffron threads,
  crushed

500 g (1 lb 2 oz) raw (green)
  prawns, shelled, deveined
  and cut in half

500 g (1 lb 2 oz) squid tubes,
  cleaned and cut into 1.5-cm
  (⅝-in) thick rings

3 tablespoons finely chopped
  fresh flat-leaf parsley

3 tablespoons finely chopped
  fresh coriander

1 preserved lemon, quartered,
  flesh discarded and skin
  finely chopped

salt and freshly ground black
  pepper

10 sheets filo pastry

150 g (5 oz) butter, melted

1 cup grated tasty cheese

1 large egg yolk, lightly
  beaten

Preheat the oven to 200°C (390°F). Grease a deep 30-cm (12-in) pizza pan.

Soak the noodles in boiling water for 5 minutes, until softened. Drain, chop
coarsely and set aside.

Pour the stock and lemon juice into a large saucepan and bring to the boil. Reduce the heat to low, add the fish and poach gently for 3–4 minutes on each side, until cooked through. Remove the fish, reserving the liquid, and flake into large chunks. Place in a large bowl and set aside.

Sauté the onion and spices in a large saucepan until softened. Increase the heat to high, add the prawns and cook for 1 minute. Add the squid and cook for 2–3 minutes, until the prawns turn pink and the squid turns white. Remove the seafood from the pan and add to the fish. Pour the reserved stock into the pan and simmer until reduced to about 2 tablespoons. Add the reduced stock, noodles, herbs and lemon to the seafood. Stir to combine and season with salt and pepper.

Brush one sheet of filo pastry with melted butter, fold in half and place in the base of the pizza pan. Repeat with another eight sheets of pastry. Arrange the sheets, overlapping, to cover the sides of the pan, leaving one-third of the pastry hanging over the edge.

Pour the seafood into the pan and sprinkle with the cheese. Fold the pastry over the filling to encase, brushing in between layers with melted butter to seal. Brush around the edge with egg yolk and lay the last sheet of filo over the top. Carefully tuck the edges under to form a round pie. Brush the top with melted butter and egg yolk. Pierce a few holes in the top with a skewer. Bake in the oven for 15–20 minutes, until crisp and golden-brown.

Veal, Lamb
& Chicken

Chicken, Morocco's most popular poultry, is usually steamed or roasted, and stuffed with various fillings such as couscous, rice, vermicelli noodles, kefta or almonds. Try making Morocco's famous chicken bastilla (page 152). This rich pie is layered with eggs, chicken and sweet roasted almonds, wrapped in crisp warka pastry and dusted with sugar and cinnamon. It takes some time to make, but it is definitely worth the effort.

In Moroccan cuisine, meat is always slow-cooked, gently spiced and heavily basted. The end result is tender, fall-off-the-bone morsels, which are eaten with the fingers or wrapped in freshly baked bread.

< Slow-cooked Veal Stew (page 140)

Slow-cooked Veal Stew

Tangia

Serves 6

1.5 kg (3 lb 5 oz) veal osso
  bucco

2 large red onions, grated

2 preserved lemons, quartered
  and deseeded

4 cloves garlic, finely chopped

1½ tablespoons ground cumin

¼ teaspoon freshly ground
  black pepper

¼ teaspoon ground turmeric

pinch of saffron threads,
  crumbled

½ teaspoon salt

120 g (4 oz) butter, cubed

Preheat the oven to 120°C (250°F).

Place the veal, onion, lemon, garlic, spices and salt in a large baking dish and toss to coat. Dot with the butter and pour in 2 cups (500 ml/17 fl oz) water. Cover with a piece of baking paper, followed by aluminium foil, and secure tightly. Cook in the oven for 8 hours, until the meat is tender and falling off the bone.

Spicy Lamb

Serves 8

1 × 2.5-kg (5 lb 5-oz) leg of lamb

150 g (5 oz) butter, softened

2 cloves garlic, crushed

2 teaspoons ground cumin

½ teaspoon freshly ground black pepper

½ teaspoon cayenne pepper

1 teaspoon salt

2 large red onions, quartered

½ bunch fresh flat-leaf parsley

½ bunch fresh lemon thyme

3 bay leaves

2 tablespoons (40 ml/1½ fl oz) olive oil

Trim the lamb of fat and make 1.5-cm (⅝-in) deep incisions into the flesh. Combine half of the butter with all of the garlic, spices and salt in a small bowl. Rub over the lamb and into the incisions, then wrap in a large piece of muslin.

One-third fill the bottom of a large steamer saucepan with water, place over high heat and bring to the boil. Arrange the onion and herbs in the top steamer section of the saucepan. Put the wrapped lamb leg on top, ensuring that it is sealed completely. (Wrap foil around the rim of the saucepan if necessary to seal.) Cover and steam the lamb for 2–2½ hours or until the meat is tender and almost falling off the bone. Remove the lamb from the steamer.

Melt the remaining butter in a large flameproof baking dish over high heat and brown the lamb on all sides. Transfer to a serving dish.

M'hammer-spiced Lamb

Serves 6

1.5 kg (3 lb 5 oz) shoulder of lamb

150 g (5 oz) butter, softened

2 cloves garlic, crushed

2 teaspoons paprika

1 teaspoon ground cumin

1 teaspoon cayenne pepper

½ teaspoon freshly ground black pepper

½ teaspoon ground turmeric

pinch of saffron threads, crumbled

1 teaspoon salt

2 large red onions, finely chopped

½ cup finely chopped fresh coriander

Trim the lamb of fat and make 1.5-cm (⅝-in) deep incisions into the flesh. Combine half of the butter with all of the garlic, spices and salt in a bowl. Rub over the lamb and into the incisions.

Put half of the onion in a large, heavy-based saucepan and sprinkle with half of the coriander. Place the lamb on top and sprinkle with the remaining onion and coriander. Pour in 1½ cups (375 ml/12½ fl oz) water and bring to the boil. Decrease the heat to low–medium and cook, basting occasionally, for 1½–2 hours, until the meat is tender and almost falling off the bone.

Melt the remaining butter in a large flameproof baking dish over high heat and brown the lamb, turning on all sides. Transfer to a serving dish and cover with aluminium foil to keep warm.

Add the butter to the remaining liquid in the saucepan. Place over medium–high heat and simmer until thickened to a sauce. Pour over the lamb.

Spiced Lamb Stuffed with Kefta

Serves 8

1 × 2-kg (4 lb 6-oz) leg of
lamb, boned

2 tablespoons (40 ml/1½ fl oz)
olive oil

1 teaspoon paprika

½ teaspoon ground cumin

salt and freshly ground black
pepper

1 large red onion, coarsely
chopped

KEFTA STUFFING

¼ cup (60 ml/2 fl oz) olive oil

1 small red onion, grated

2 cloves garlic, crushed

½ teaspoon ground cumin

½ teaspoon ground cinnamon

¼ teaspoon ground ginger

¼ teaspoon paprika

pinch of freshly ground black
pepper

pinch of cayenne pepper

¼ teaspoon salt

125 g (4½ oz) lamb mince

100 g (3½ oz) chicken livers,
finely chopped

2 tablespoons finely chopped
fresh flat-leaf parsley

2 tablespoons finely chopped
fresh coriander

1 large egg

Trim the lamb of any excess fat. Make a cut into the flesh, but not all the
way through, and butterfly the meat, opening it out so that it can wrap and
encase the filling.

Meanwhile, to make the kefta stuffing, heat the oil in a medium-sized frying pan over low–medium heat. Add the onion, garlic, spices and salt and sauté until softened and fragrant. Remove from the heat and transfer to a medium-sized bowl. Add the mince, liver, parsley, coriander and egg and mix well to combine.

Spread the stuffing over the inside of the butterflied lamb. Wrap the meat around to encase the kefta stuffing and tie up with kitchen string.

Combine the oil, paprika and cumin and rub over the lamb. Season with salt and pepper. Put the onion in the base of a large saucepan and place the lamb on top. Pour in 1 cup (250 ml/8½ fl oz) water and bring to the boil. Decrease the heat to low, cover and cook for 1½–2 hours, until tender.

Preheat the oven to 200°C (390°F).

Take the lamb out of the saucepan and transfer to a large baking dish. Bake in the oven for 15–20 minutes, until browned.

Slow-roasted Leg of Lamb

Mechoui

Serves 8

1 x 2.5-kg (5 lb 5-oz) leg of lamb
120 g (4 oz) butter, softened
3 cloves garlic, crushed
1 tablespoon paprika
2 teaspoons ground cumin
2 teaspoons ground coriander

½ teaspoon freshly ground
 black pepper
½ teaspoon cayenne pepper
½ teaspoon ground cinnamon
1 teaspoon salt

Preheat the oven to 220°C (420°F).

Trim the lamb of any excess fat and make 1.5-cm (⅝-in) deep incisions into the flesh.

Combine the butter, garlic, spices and salt in a bowl. Rub over the lamb and into the incisions. Place the lamb leg in a large baking dish and pour in 1 cup (250 ml/8½ fl oz) water. Bake in the oven on the top shelf for 20 minutes.

Move the lamb to the middle shelf, reduce the heat to 160°C (320°F) and bake for a further 3 hours, until the meat is tender and almost falling off the bone. Baste with the pan juices every 15 minutes to keep the lamb moist and flavoursome.

Lamb with Hard-boiled Eggs & Almonds

Tafaya

Serves 6

1 kg (2 lb 3 oz) boneless lamb shoulder or leg

¼ (60 ml/2 fl oz) olive oil

1 large red onion, grated

2 cloves garlic, finely chopped

1½ teaspoons ground ginger

½ teaspoon ground cinnamon

¼ teaspoon freshly ground black pepper

pinch of saffron threads, crumbled

½ teaspoon salt

½ cup finely chopped fresh coriander

2 tablespoons (40 ml/1½ fl oz) vegetable oil

1 cup blanched almonds

6 hard-boiled eggs, peeled and halved lengthways

Trim the lamb of sinew and excess fat and cut into large cubes of approximately 5 cm (2 in).

Heat the olive oil in a large, heavy-based saucepan or flameproof dish over medium heat. Add the lamb, onion, garlic, spices and salt and cook for 5–10 minutes, stirring occasionally, until the lamb is browned and the spices are fragrant. Pour in 2 cups (500 ml/17 fl oz) water and bring to the boil. Reduce the heat to low, cover and cook for 1½ hours. **>**

Add the coriander and stir to combine. Cook for a further 30 minutes, until the meat is tender.

Meanwhile, heat the vegetable oil in a medium-sized frying pan over low–medium heat. Add the almonds and cook until golden brown. Remove using a slotted spoon and drain on paper towel.

Arrange the lamb on a serving plate and cover with sauce. Decorate with the egg halves and scatter with the almonds.

Lamb Stuffed with Couscous

Serves 8

1 × 2-kg (4 lb 6-oz) leg of lamb, boned

80 g (3 oz) butter, softened

2 cloves garlic, crushed

1 teaspoon paprika

½ teaspoon ground cumin

¼ teaspoon freshly ground black pepper

¼ teaspoon cayenne pepper

½ teaspoon salt

COUSCOUS STUFFING

¾ cup couscous

1¼ cups (310 ml/10½ fl oz) water with 1 teaspoon salt

1 tablespoon (20 ml/¾ fl oz) olive oil

¼ cup raisins

1 tablespoon (20 ml/¾ fl oz) vegetable oil

¼ cup slivered almonds

1 tablespoons (20 g/¾ oz) butter

½ teaspoon ground cinnamon

½ teaspoon ground cumin

¼ teaspoon ground ginger

2 tablespoons finely chopped fresh flat-leaf parsley

salt and freshly ground black pepper

To make the couscous stuffing, follow the method for traditional Moroccan couscous on page 54, using ½ cup (125 ml/4 fl oz) salted water in the first step. Add the remaining salted water and the olive oil during step two, or follow the packet instructions for instant couscous.

Meanwhile, place the raisins in a small bowl and cover with boiling water. Set aside for 10 minutes to plump up. Drain.

Heat the vegetable oil in a medium-sized frying pan over low–medium heat. Add the almonds and cook until golden brown. Remove using a slotted spoon and drain on paper towel.

Add the butter, raisins, almonds, spices and parsley to the couscous and mix in using your fingers. Season with salt and pepper.

Preheat the oven to 220°C (420°F).

Spread the prepared couscous over the butterflied lamb. Wrap the meat around to encase and truss with kitchen string.

Place any excess couscous in a small baking tray and cover with foil, ready to heat in the oven 20 minutes before the lamb is ready to serve.

Combine the butter, garlic, spices and salt and rub over the lamb. Place the lamb leg in a large baking dish and pour in 1 cup (250 ml/8½ fl oz) water. Bake in the oven on the top shelf for 20 minutes. Move the lamb to the middle shelf, reduce the heat to 180°C (360°F) and bake for a further 2–2½ hours or until the meat is tender and almost falling off the bone. Baste with the pan juices occasionally to keep the lamb moist and flavoursome.

Chicken Bastilla

Serves 8–10

1 × 1.5-kg (3 lb 5-oz) chicken, wings discarded

3 medium-sized brown onions, roughly chopped

2 teaspoons ground ginger

1 teaspoon ground turmeric

pinch of saffron threads

salt and freshly ground black pepper

¾ cup (180 ml/6 fl oz) vegetable oil

1 tablespoon (20 g/¾ oz) butter

3 cups roughly chopped fresh flat-leaf parsley

3 tablespoons roughly chopped fresh coriander

2 tablespoons (30 g/1 oz) sugar

1 teaspoon ground cinnamon, plus extra to garnish

10 large eggs, lightly beaten, plus 1 large egg yolk

10 sheets filo pastry

100 g (3½ oz) butter, melted

icing sugar, to garnish

ALMOND FILLING

⅓ cup (80 ml/3 fl oz) vegetable oil

3 cups blanched almonds

2 tablespoons (30 g/1 oz) sugar

Place the chicken, onion, spices, salt, oil and butter in a large saucepan and turn to coat. Cover and cook over low–medium heat for 30 minutes. Pour in 1½ cups (375 ml/10½ fl oz) water, cover and cook for 30–45 minutes.

To make the filling, heat the oil in a frying pan over low–medium heat. Add almonds and cook until golden. Drain on paper towel and allow to cool. **>**

Blend the almonds and sugar in a food processor to make fine crumbs.

Remove the chicken from the saucepan, reserving the liquid, and set aside to cool slightly. Strip the meat off the bones, roughly shred and set aside.

Heat the reserved cooking liquid over low–medium heat. Add the herbs, sugar and cinnamon and stir to combine. Gradually pour in the beaten egg, stirring constantly until thickened. Take off the heat and set aside.

Preheat the oven to 200°C (390°F). Grease a deep 30-cm (12-in) pizza pan. Brush one sheet of filo pastry with melted butter, fold in half and place in the base of the pizza pan. Repeat with another eight sheets of pastry. Arrange the sheets, overlapping, to cover the sides of the pan, leaving one-third of the pastry hanging over the edge.

Pour the egg mixture into the pastry case. Create a second layer with the chicken and a final layer with the almond mixture. Wrap the overhanging pastry over the filling to encase, brushing in between layers with butter to seal. Brush around the edge with egg yolk and lay the final sheet of filo over the top. Carefully tuck the edges under to form a round pie. Brush the top with butter and egg yolk. Pierce a few holes in the top to allow the steam to escape. Bake in the oven for 15–20 minutes, until crisp and golden brown.

To decorate, dust the top of the pie with icing sugar and create a lattice pattern with thin lines of cinnamon.

Chicken Stuffed with Couscous

Serves 4

1 × 1.5-kg (3 lb 5-oz) chicken

1 large red onion, grated

2 tablespoons honey

2 tablespoons (40 g/1½ oz) butter

1½ teaspoons ground cinnamon

½ teaspoon ground ginger

pinch of saffron threads, crumbled

COUSCOUS STUFFING

1 cup couscous

1 teaspoon salt

1 tablespoon (20 ml/¾ fl oz) olive oil

¾ cup raisins

2 tablespoons (40 ml/1½ fl oz) vegetable oil

1 cup (140 g/5 oz) blanched almonds

2 tablespoons (40 g/1½ oz) butter

2 teaspoons caster sugar

1 teaspoon ground cinnamon

salt and ground black pepper

Preheat the oven to 200°C (390°F).

To make the couscous stuffing, follow the preparation for traditional Moroccan couscous on page 54 using ½ cup (125 ml/4 fl oz) salted water in step one and ¾ cup (180ml/6 fl oz) water and the olive oil in step two, or follow packet instructions for instant couscous. >

Meanwhile, place the raisins in a small bowl and cover with boiling water. Set aside for 10 minutes to plump up. Drain.

Heat the vegetable oil in a medium-sized frying pan over low–medium heat. Add the almonds and cook until golden. Drain on paper towel and coarsely chop.

Add the butter, almonds, raisins, sugar and cinnamon to the couscous and rub through using your fingers to separate the grains. Add seasoning.

Wash the chicken and the cavity thoroughly with cold running water and pat dry with paper towel. Stuff the cavity of the chicken with the prepared couscous. To prevent the stuffing from falling out, fold over the two flaps of skin and secure using toothpicks. Truss the legs together using kitchen string. (Place any excess couscous in a small baking tray and cover with foil to heat through in the oven 20 minutes before the chicken is ready.)

Combine the onion, honey, butter and spices in a bowl. Spread this mixture over the base of a large baking dish. Place the chicken on top and pour in 1¼ cups (310 ml/ 10½ fl oz) water. Cover with aluminium foil and cook in the oven for 45 minutes. Uncover the chicken and return to the oven, basting occasionally, for a further 45 minutes or until the juices run clear from the thickest part of the thigh when tested.

Sweet Tomato Chicken

Serves 4

1 × 1.5-kg (3 lb 5-oz) chicken

120 g (4 oz) butter, cubed

1 clove garlic, finely chopped

½ teaspoon ground ginger

¼ teaspoon freshly ground
  black pepper

pinch of saffron threads,
  crumbled

½ teaspoon salt

1 large red onion, grated

15 medium-sized tomatoes,
  peeled, deseeded and
  coarsely chopped

3 tablespoons honey

2 teaspoons ground cinnamon

2 tablespoons (40 ml/1½ fl oz)
  vegetable oil

⅔ cup blanched almonds

Wash the chicken and the cavity thoroughly with cold running water and pat dry with paper towel.

Combine the butter, garlic, spices and salt in a bowl. Rub over the chicken and inside the cavity. Put half of the onion and tomato in the base of a large saucepan, big enough to hold the chicken. Place the chicken on top and cover with the remaining onion and tomato. Cover and cook over low–medium heat for 1½ hours or until the juices run clear from the thickest part of the thigh when tested. Remove the chicken, transfer to a plate, cover and set aside to keep warm. >

Add the honey and cinnamon to the saucepan and cook over low heat, stirring occasionally, for 20–30 minutes, until all of the liquid has evaporated.

Meanwhile, heat the oil in a medium-sized frying pan over low–medium heat. Add the almonds and cook until golden brown. Remove using a slotted spoon, drain on paper towel and coarsely chop.

Return the chicken to the saucepan to heat through, turning to coat in the tomato jam. Serve scattered with almonds.

Chicken Stuffed with Kefta

Serves 4

1 × 1.5-kg (3 lb 5-oz) chicken

2 tablespoons (40 g/1½ oz) butter

½ teaspoon paprika

½ teaspoon salt

¼ teaspoon freshly ground black pepper

KEFTA STUFFING

2 tablespoons (40 ml/1½ fl oz) olive oil

1 large red onion, grated

1 clove garlic, finely chopped

1 teaspoon ground cumin

1 teaspoon paprika

¼ teaspoon freshly ground black pepper

¼ teaspoon salt

200 g (7 oz) beef mince

juice of ½ lemon

3 large eggs, lightly beaten

3 tablespoons finely chopped fresh flat-leaf parsley

To make the kefta stuffing, heat oil in a large frying pan over low–medium heat. Add the onion, garlic, spices and salt and sauté until softened and fragrant. Add the mince and cook, stirring to break up, for 5 minutes or until browned. Pour in ¼ cup (60 ml/2 fl oz) water and lemon juice and bring to the boil. Simmer for 2 minutes or until the liquid has reduced by half. Pour in the egg and cook, stirring, until set. Add the parsley and stir to combine. Remove from the heat and set aside to cool slightly.

Preheat the oven to 200°C (390°F).

Wash the chicken and the cavity thoroughly with cold running water and pat dry with paper towel.

Combine the butter, paprika, salt and pepper in a small bowl. Rub over the chicken and inside the cavity. Stuff the cavity of the chicken with the prepared kefta. To prevent the stuffing from falling out, fold over the two flaps of skin and secure using toothpicks. Truss the legs together using kitchen string.

Bake in the oven for 1½ hours, basting occasionally, until the juices run clear from the thickest part of the thigh when tested.

Roast Chicken with Preserved Lemon & Olives

Serves 4

1 × 1.5-kg (3 lb 5-oz) chicken

2 preserved lemons

150 g (5 oz) butter, softened

2 cloves garlic, crushed

1½ teaspoons ground ginger

¼ teaspoon ground turmeric

pinch of saffron threads, crumbled

salt and freshly ground black pepper

2 large onions, thickly sliced

¾ cup red or green olives

Preheat the oven to 200°C (390°F).

Wash the chicken and the cavity thoroughly with cold running water and pat dry with paper towel. Stuff the cavity of the chicken with one of the preserved lemons and truss the legs together using kitchen string.

Discard the flesh of the remaining preserved lemon and finely chop the skin. Combine the lemon, butter, garlic and spices in a small bowl. Rub the butter mixture over the chicken. Season with salt and pepper.

Place the chicken in a large baking dish. Scatter the onion and olives around the chicken and pour in 1½ cups (375 ml/12½ fl oz) water. Cover with aluminium foil and bake for 45 minutes. Uncover and cook, basting occasionally, for a further 45 minutes, until the juices run clear from the thickest part of the thigh when tested.

Chicken Stuffed with Spiced Rice

Serves 4

1 × 1.5-kg (3 lb 5-oz) chicken

2 tablespoons (40 ml/1½ fl oz) olive oil

1 teaspoon paprika

salt and freshly ground black pepper

RICE STUFFING

½ cup long-grain rice, rinsed

2 tablespoons (40 ml/1½ fl oz) olive oil

1 tablespoon (20 g/¾ oz) butter

1 large red onion, finely chopped

2 cloves garlic, finely chopped

1½ teaspoons paprika

1 teaspoon ground cumin

¼ teaspoon ground turmeric

¼ teaspoon cayenne pepper

2 chicken livers, finely chopped

¼ cup finely chopped fresh flat-leaf parsley

juice of ½ lemon

salt and freshly ground black pepper

To make the rice stuffing, place a medium-sized saucepan of water on high heat and bring to the boil. Add the rice and cook for 10–15 minutes, until just tender.

Preheat the oven to 200°C (390°F).

Heat the oil and butter in a large frying pan over low–medium heat. Add the onion, garlic and spices and cook until softened and fragrant. Add the chicken livers and cook for a further 2–3 minutes, until golden. Combine the rice, parsley and lemon juice and season with salt and pepper.

Wash the chicken and the cavity thoroughly with cold running water and pat dry with paper towel. Stuff the cavity of the chicken with the prepared rice. To prevent the stuffing from falling out, fold over the two flaps of skin and secure using toothpicks. Truss the legs together using kitchen string.

Put the chicken in a large baking dish. Drizzle with the oil, sprinkle with the paprika and season with salt and pepper. Pour 1½ cups (375 ml/12½ fl oz) water into the baking dish. Cover with aluminium foil and bake for 45 minutes. Uncover and cook, basting occasionally, for a further 45 minutes, until the juices run clear from the thickest part of the thigh when tested.

Chicken Stuffed with Almond Paste

Serves 4

1 × 1.5-kg (3 lb 5-oz) chicken

1 tablespoon (20 g/¾ oz) butter

½ teaspoon ground cinnamon

½ teaspoon ground ginger

½ teaspoon salt

¼ teaspoon freshly ground black pepper

pinch of saffron threads, crushed

1 large red onion, grated

2 tablespoons finely chopped fresh flat-leaf parsley

juice of ½ lemon

ALMOND STUFFING

2 tablespoons (40 ml/1½ fl oz) vegetable oil

1⅓ cups blanched almonds

¼ cup (55 g/2 oz) caster sugar

2 tablespoons (40 g/1½ oz) butter

½ teaspoon ground cinnamon

Wash the chicken and the cavity thoroughly with cold running water and pat dry with paper towel.

Combine the butter, cinnamon, ginger, salt, pepper and saffron in a bowl. Rub over the chicken and inside the cavity. Combine the onion and parsley and put in the base of a saucepan big enough to hold the chicken. Place the chicken on top and pour in the lemon juice and ¼ cup (60 ml/2 fl oz) water. Cover and cook over low–medium heat for 45 minutes.

Meanwhile, to prepare the almond stuffing, heat the oil in a medium-sized frying pan over low–medium heat. Add the almonds and cook until golden. Remove using a slotted spoon and drain on paper towel. Blend the almonds, sugar, butter and cinnamon together in a food processor to make a smooth paste.

Preheat the oven to 200°C (390°F).

Remove the chicken from the saucepan and place in a deep baking dish. Pour any remaining cooking liquid around and over the chicken. Stuff the chicken with the prepared almond paste, being careful not to burn yourself. To prevent the stuffing from falling out, fold over the two flaps of skin and secure using toothpicks. Truss the legs together using kitchen string.

Bake in the oven for 30–45 minutes, basting occasionally, until the juices run clear from the thickest part of the thigh when tested.

Chicken Stuffed with Vermicelli

Serves 4

1 × 1.5-kg (3 lb 5-oz) chicken

1 large red onion, finely chopped

¼ cup (60 ml/2 fl oz) olive oil

2 cloves garlic, finely chopped

½ teaspoon ground ginger

pinch of saffron threads

salt and freshly ground black pepper

VERMICELLI STUFFING

100 g (3½ oz) vermicelli rice noodles

2 tablespoons (40 ml/1½ fl oz) olive oil

2 cloves garlic, crushed

1 teaspoon ground ginger

1 teaspoon ground cumin

½ teaspoon ground turmeric

2 tablespoons finely chopped fresh flat-leaf parsley

2 tablespoons finely chopped fresh coriander

salt and freshly ground black pepper

Preheat the oven to 200°C (390°F).

To make the vermicelli stuffing, soak the noodles in boiling water for 5 minutes, until softened. Drain and roughly chop. Combine the noodles, oil, garlic and spices in a bowl. Add the parsley and coriander, mix and season with salt and pepper. >

Wash the chicken and the cavity thoroughly with cold running water and pat dry with paper towel. Stuff the cavity of the chicken with the prepared stuffing. To prevent the stuffing from falling out, fold over the two flaps of skin and secure using toothpicks. Truss the legs together using kitchen string.

Place the onion in the base of a large baking dish and the chicken on top. Combine the oil, garlic, ginger and saffron in a small bowl. Pour over the chicken and rub to coat. Season with salt and pepper. Pour 1½ cups (375 ml/12½ fl oz) water into the baking dish. Cover with aluminium foil and cook in the oven for 45 minutes. Uncover the chicken and return to the oven to cook, basting occasionally, for a further 45 minutes, until the juices run clear from the thickest part of the thigh when tested.

M'qualli-spiced Chicken

Serves 4

1 × 1.5-kg (3 lb 5-oz) chicken, butterflied

1 medium-sized red onion, grated

¼ cup (60 ml/2 fl oz) olive oil

2 tablespoons (40 ml/1½ fl oz) lemon juice

2 teaspoons ground ginger

1 preserved lemon, finely chopped

2 pinches saffron threads, crumbled

½ teaspoon salt

¼ teaspoon freshly ground black pepper

2 lemons, cut into wedges

Insert two metal skewers through the chicken, beginning at the thickest part of each breast and going all the way through to the thigh. This will ensure the chicken stays splayed. Score the chicken in the thickest part of the leg to help it cook evenly.

Combine the remaining ingredients, except the lemon wedges, in a small bowl. Coat the chicken in this spice mixture and place in the refrigerator to marinate for at least 6 hours or overnight.

Preheat barbecue or chargrill to medium–high. Cook the chicken, basting with the marinade, for 10–15 minutes on each side, until the juices run clear from the thickest part of the thigh when tested. Remove the skewers, then cut the chicken into portions and serve with lemon wedges.

Sweets

In Morocco, women traditionally do most of the cooking and culinary knowledge is passed down through the generations. Great pride is taken in what is prepared and sweet-making is no exception. Women gather together in each other's houses to make large batches of delicious pastries. A decadent bounty is always produced and divided at the end of the day, keeping households well stocked for visitors who may stop by.

Moroccan sweets and pastries are rarely eaten as part of a meal, except during the month of Ramadan and at celebrations or feasts. Instead they are enjoyed as afternoon treats. Platters of seasonal fresh fruit are traditionally served at the end of most meals.

‹ Doughnuts (page 174)

Doughnuts

Sfinges

Makes 20

2 teaspoons dry yeast

1 teaspoon caster sugar, plus
extra for dusting (optional)

1 cup (250 ml/8½ fl oz)
lukewarm water

2½ cups (375 g/13 oz) plain
flour

1 teaspoon salt

vegetable oil, for deep-frying

Combine the yeast, sugar and ¼ cup (60 ml/2 fl oz) of the water in a small bowl. Cover with a clean tea towel and set aside in a warm place for 10 minutes or until the yeast begins to bubble.

Sift the flour and salt into a bowl and make a well in the centre. Pour in the yeast mixture and the remaining water and gradually stir into the flour to form a dough.

Knead the dough for 10–15 minutes, until the dough becomes, soft, loose and elastic. Place in a lightly oiled bowl and cover with a clean tea towel. Put in a warm place for 1 hour or until doubled in size.

Punch out the dough to remove all the air. Divide into 20 even-sized balls and place on a lightly oiled tray. Using your index finger, make a hole in the centre of one of the balls and swing the dough around your finger to make a large, loose ring. Swing and stretch the dough until you can fit your three middle fingers in the centre. Lay the dough ring on another lightly oiled tray. Repeat with the remaining dough. Cover with a clean tea towel and set aside in a warm place for 20 minutes or until doubled in size.

Half-fill a large, heavy-based saucepan with oil, for deep-frying. Heat the oil to 180°C (360°F) or until a piece of bread browns in 15 seconds when tested.

Carefully drop the rings, a few at a time, into the oil and deep-fry in batches, turning occasionally, until puffed and golden brown. Remove using a slotted spoon and drain on paper towel.

Serve immediately, sprinkled with caster sugar (if using).

Almond Batons

Makes 25

1 egg white, lightly beaten

¼ cup sesame seeds

PASTRY

½ cup (75 g/2½ oz) plain flour

2 teaspoons icing sugar

pinch of salt

¼ cup (60 ml/2 fl oz) double
  cream

ALMOND FILLING

¾ cup (75 g/2½ oz) ground
  almonds

⅓ cup (55 g/2 oz) icing sugar

½ teaspoon ground cinnamon

2 teaspoons softened butter

1 tablespoon (20 ml/¾ fl oz)
  orange-blossom water

To make the pastry, combine the flour, icing sugar and salt in a medium-sized bowl. Add the cream and stir to combine. Knead to make a dough. Wrap in cling wrap and refrigerate for 30 minutes.

Preheat the oven to 170°C (340°F). Line a baking tray with baking paper.

For the filling, combine almonds, sugar and cinnamon. Add butter and orange-blossom water, and knead to a paste. Roll into 1-cm (⅜-in) thick logs.

Roll the pastry out to 2 mm (⅛ in) thick. Place a stick of filling on the pastry, wrap to enclose and press to seal. Repeat with the remaining filling and pastry. Cut into 5 cm (2 in) batons. Dip the ends in egg white then sesame seeds. Bake for 15–20 minutes, until just cooked but still pale in colour.

Honeyed Pastry Ribbons

Chebbakia

Makes 25

vegetable oil, for deep-frying

¼ cup sesame seeds, toasted

PASTRY

¾ cup sesame seeds, toasted

1 teaspoon dry yeast

pinch of saffron threads,
    finely crushed

3 tablespoons (60 ml/2 fl oz)
    lukewarm water

2 cups (300 g/10½ oz) plain
    flour

½ teaspoon ground cinnamon

pinch of salt

2 tablespoons (40 ml/1½ fl oz)
    olive oil

2 tablespoons (40 g/1½ oz)
    butter, melted

1½ tablespoons (30 ml/1 fl oz)
    white-wine vinegar

1 large egg, lightly beaten

2 tablespoons (40 ml/1½ fl oz)
    orange-blossom water

HONEY DIP

2 cups (500 ml/ 17 fl oz) honey

3 tablespoons (60 ml/2 fl oz)
    orange-blossom water

To make the pastry, place the sesame seeds in a food processor and finely grind to a flour-like consistency. Mix the yeast, saffron and water in a cup and set aside.

Lightly oil a baking tray. ❯

Combine the ground sesame seeds, flour, cinnamon and salt in a medium-sized bowl. Make a well in the centre and add the olive oil, butter, vinegar and egg. Rub the mixture together using your fingertips to create a fine texture, resembling breadcrumbs. Add the yeast mixture and the orange-blossom water, mixing until a dough forms. Knead for 10–15 minutes, or until it becomes elastic. Divide the dough into five even-sized balls and place on the baking tray. Loosely cover with cling wrap and set aside to rest in a warm place for 20 minutes.

Lightly flour a clean work surface and roll out a portion of dough to less than 5 mm (¼ in) thick. Cut out 10-cm (4-in) squares using a fluted pastry wheel. Make four cuts the same length across the centre of each square, leaving a 1.5-cm (⅝-in) border, to create five even strips connected down two edges.

To shape the ribbons, gently hold the first, third and fifth strips with your fingers and lift the square off the bench, allowing the remaining two strips to hang down. Press the two side corners closest to you together firmly to secure, to prevent them from coming apart when cooking. Feed the pressed corners up through the centre hole you have created between the strips (almost as if you are turning the chebbakia inside out) to create a flower-like shape. Place on the lightly oiled tray and set aside. Any pastry scraps can be re-kneaded and re-rolled once to create additional pastries.

To make the honey dip, pour the honey and orange-blossom water into a large frying pan and warm over low heat. If the honey gets too hot and begins to boil, add a little additional orange-blossom water and reduce the temperature slightly.

Pour enough vegetable oil into a large frying pan for deep-frying. Heat to 180°C (360°F) or until a piece of bread browns in 15 seconds when tested.

Deep-fry the pastries in batches for 3 minutes on each side, until golden brown and crisp. Remove each batch using a slotted spoon, drain for a few seconds, then place directly in the prepared honey dip. Hold the pastries down in the honey for 1 minute and turn until fully coated. Leave to soak up the honey for 2–3 minutes. Remove using a slotted spoon, drain slightly and place on a baking tray. Sprinkle immediately with the toasted sesame seeds.

✵ Chebbakia can be found everywhere in Morocco during the month of Ramadan. They are traditionally eaten alongside harira soup (page 32) to break the fast after the sun has set.

✵ Chebbakia and other Moroccan pastries are usually made in bulk with the help of many women, either family members or neighbours, and then divided up to share. Although it is possible to make and shape the chebbakia on your own, it is recommended that you have help for the final stages of frying and dipping in honey as the transferring needs to be done quickly for optimum results.

Almond Briouats

Makes 30

640 g (2 lb) ground almonds

¼ cup (55 g/2 oz) caster sugar

100 g (3½ oz) butter, softened

⅓ cup (80 ml/3 fl oz) orange-blossom water

½ teaspoon ground cinnamon

10 large spring-roll wrappers

2 large egg yolks, lightly beaten

vegetable oil, for deep-frying

HONEY DIP

2 cups (500 ml/17 fl oz) honey

3 tablespoons (60 ml/2 fl oz) orange-blossom water

In a medium-sized bowl, combine the ground almonds, sugar, butter, orange-blossom water and cinnamon. Knead, then roll the mixture into 30 even-sized balls.

Place a spring-roll wrapper on a clean bench and cut into three even lengths. Place a ball of filling at the end of each length and flatten slightly. Encase the filling in the wrapper, folding the wrapper back and forth and flattening each time, to create a triangular parcel. Brush the ends with egg yolk and press to seal. Repeat the process with the remaining filling and pastry.

Pour enough oil into a large frying pan for deep-frying. Heat to 180°C (360°F) or until a piece of bread browns in 15 seconds when tested. **>**

To make the honey dip, pour the honey and orange-blossom water into a large frying pan and warm over low heat. If the honey gets too hot and begins to boil, add a little additional orange-blossom water and reduce the temperature slightly.

Deep-fry the briouats in batches for 1–2 minutes on each side, until golden brown and crisp. Remove using a slotted spoon, drain for a few seconds and place directly in the prepared honey dip. Hold down in the honey for 1 minute and turn until fully coated. Leave to soak up the honey for 3–5 minutes. Remove using a slotted spoon, allowing excess honey to drain, and place on a baking tray.

❈ Briouats can be prepared up to the cooking stage and frozen in an airtight container for up to 2–3 months.

Almond-filled Pastry Snake

M'hanncha

Makes 1 large snake

9 sheets filo pastry

3 tablespoons (60 g/2 oz) butter, melted

1 egg yolk

1 tablespoon coarsely chopped slivered almonds

ALMOND FILLING

1⅓ cup (135 g/4¾ oz) ground almonds

¾ cup (120 g/4 oz) icing sugar

1 teaspoon ground cinnamon

2 tablespoons (40 ml/1⅓ fl oz) orange-blossom water

1½ tablespoons (30 g/1 oz) butter, melted

HONEY SYRUP

2 tablespoons honey, warmed

1 tablespoon (20 ml/¾ fl oz) orange-blossom water

To make the almond filling, combine the ground almonds, icing sugar and cinnamon in a bowl. Add the orange-blossom water and butter and stir to combine. Divide the filling into three even-sized portions and shape into logs, slightly shorter than the width of a sheet of filo pastry.

Preheat the oven to 180°C (360°F). Line a baking tray with baking paper.

Lay a sheet of filo pastry on a clean bench and brush with melted butter. Add another two layers of filo, brushing with butter in between each layer. Keep the remaining filo covered with a damp, clean tea towel to prevent it from drying out. **>**

Place a log of filling across the long edge of the prepared pastry and roll up loosely to enclose. Repeat the process with the remaining filling and filo sheets.

Place one pastry log on the prepared baking tray seam-side down and curl into a tight spiral, pinching the centre end closed. Wrap the remaining logs, one at a time, around the spiral, joining the ends together, to create a coiled snake. Brush the top with the remaining melted butter.

Combine the egg yolk and 1 tablespoon (20 ml/¾ fl oz) water in a cup and brush over the top of the pastry coil. Sprinkle with the slivered almonds and bake in the oven for 30–35 minutes or until crisp and golden brown.

Meanwhile, to make the honey syrup, heat the honey and orange-blossom water together in a small saucepan.

Remove the pastry snake from the oven and brush with the honey syrup. Set aside to cool slightly.

Serve warm or at room temperature.

Gazelle's Horns

Makes 36

ALMOND FILLING

360 g (13½ oz) ground
  almonds

½ cup (80 g/3 oz) icing sugar

1 teaspoon ground cinnamon

2 tablespoons (40 g/1½ oz)
  unsalted butter, melted and
  cooled

1 tablespoon (20 ml/¾ fl oz)
  orange-blossom water

PASTRY

1½ cups (225 g/8 oz) plain flour

2 tablespoons (20 g/¾ oz) icing
  sugar, plus extra for dusting
  (optional)

2 tablespoons (40 g/1½ oz)
  butter, melted

2 tablespoons (40 ml/1½ fl oz)
  orange-blossom water

To make the almond filling, combine the ground almonds, icing sugar and cinnamon in a small bowl. Add the butter and orange-blossom water and stir to combine. Divide the filling into four and place in the refrigerator for 10 minutes to cool.

Meanwhile, to make the pastry, sift the flour and icing sugar into a bowl. Pour in the butter, then gradually pour in ⅓ cup (80 ml/3 fl oz) water and the orange-blossom water, stirring until a sticky dough begins to form. Knead the dough, punching into it with your fists for 15–20 minutes, until it is smooth and elastic and comes away from the bowl easily. Divide into four, then shape into blocks and refrigerate for 10 minutes. **>**

Preheat the oven to 150°C (300°F). Line a baking tray with baking paper.

Divide each portion of almond filling into 9 even-sized balls, then shape into tapered logs and set aside.

Roll out one portion of dough to make a long 10-cm (4-in) wide strip. Lay a log of filling across the shortest end, leaving a 5-cm (2-in) border. Moisten around the filling with water and fold the pastry over to enclose the filling, pressing with your fingers to seal. Cut around the edge, gently shape into a crescent and place on the prepared baking tray. Make a few holes in the top using a toothpick to prevent the pastry from cracking. Repeat the process with the remaining dough and filling.

Bake in the oven for 10–15 minutes, until just cooked but still pale in colour. Transfer to a wire rack to cool completely. Dust with icing sugar (if using).

Crisp Almond & Cream Layers

Keneffa

Serves 4–6

vegetable oil, for deep-frying

1 cup whole blanched almonds

9 spring roll wrappers

¼ cup (55 g/2 oz) caster sugar

CRÈME PÂTISSIÈRE

1.5 L (3 pt 3 fl oz) milk

1 vanilla bean, split in half lengthways and seeds scraped

4 large egg yolks

¼ cup (55 g/2 oz) caster sugar

2 tablespoons (30 g/1 oz) plain flour

1 tablespoon (20 ml/¾ fl oz) rosewater

To make the crème patissière, place the milk and vanilla bean and seeds in a medium-sized saucepan and bring to scalding point. Remove from the heat and set aside.

Beat the egg yolks and sugar together in a medium-sized bowl using an electric mixer, until pale and thick. Stir in the flour. Gradually add the hot milk, stirring with a wooden spoon to incorporate. Return to the pan and cook over low–medium heat, stirring continuously, until thickened enough to coat the back of the spoon. Discard the vanilla bean and stir in the rose-water. Take off the heat, cover with a piece of baking paper to prevent a skin from forming and set aside to cool slightly. >

Pour enough oil into a large frying pan for deep-frying. Heat the oil to 180°C (360°F) or until a piece of bread browns in 15 seconds when tested.

Deep-fry the almonds for 2 minutes or until golden brown. Remove using a slotted spoon and place on paper towel to drain and cool.

Cut the spring roll wrappers into 20-cm (8-in) rounds. Deep-fry until golden brown and crisp. Remove from the oil and drain on paper towel.

Blend the almonds and sugar in a food processor until coarsely chopped.

To assemble, arrange three spring roll discs on a large serving plate. Sprinkle with one-third of the almond mixture. Thin the crème patissière with a little warm milk if necessary and pour a layer over the top. Cover with another three discs and repeat the process, finishing with a sprinkling of nuts on top. Serve any remaining crème patissière on the side.

✳ Keneffa refers to crispy pastry sheets made with different cream fiillings. A common Moroccan treat.

Sesame Biscuits

Ghoriba behla

Makes 30

¼ cup sesame seeds, toasted

1¾ cups (260 g/9½ oz) plain flour

⅓ cup (55 g/2 oz) icing sugar

½ teaspoon dry yeast

pinch of salt

100 g (3½ oz) butter, melted

¼ cup (60 ml/2 fl oz) vegetable oil

½ teaspoon vanilla extract

Preheat the oven to 170°C (340°F). Line a baking tray with baking paper.

Place the sesame seeds in a food processor and finely grind. Combine with the flour, icing sugar, yeast and salt in a medium-sized bowl. Add the butter, oil and vanilla and rub together using your fingertips to create a fine texture resembling breadcrumbs. Squeeze golfball-sized portions of the mixture in the palm of your hand to bind the mixture together. Gently roll into a ball. Transfer the ball back and forth from one palm to the other to flatten slightly. (The mixture is quite crumbly and it can take a little practice to shape.)

Place the shaped dough on the prepared tray and bake in the oven for 15 minutes or until golden brown. Leave to cool on the tray for 10 minutes, then transfer to a wire rack to cool completely.

Date Crescents

Makes 20

1 large egg white, lightly
  beaten

icing sugar, for dusting

PASTRY

3⅓ cups (500 g/1 lb 2 oz) plain
  flour

¼ cup (40 g/1½ oz) icing
  sugar

250 g (9 oz) butter, cubed

⅓ cup (80 ml/3 fl oz) milk

DATE FILLING

500 g (1 lb 2 oz) pitted dried
  dates

1 tablespoon (10 g/⅜ oz)
  ground almonds

1 tablespoon (20 ml/¾ fl oz)
  orange-blossom water

2 teaspoons butter

1 teaspoon ground cinnamon

To make the pastry, sift the flour and icing sugar together into a medium-sized bowl. Rub in the butter, using your fingertips, until the mixture resembles fine breadcrumbs. Add the milk, a little at a time, until a dough forms. Shape into a ball, cover with cling wrap and refrigerate for 30 minutes. >

Meanwhile, to make the date filling, place the dates in a small saucepan and cover with ½ cup (125 ml/4 fl oz) boiling water. Set aside to soak for 10 minutes or until softened. Add a further ¼ cup (60 ml/2 fl oz) water and cook, stirring, over low heat for 10 minutes or until a paste forms. Add the ground almonds, orange-blossom water, butter and cinnamon and stir to combine. Transfer to a small bowl and set aside to cool.

Preheat the oven to 160°C (320°F). Line 2 baking trays with baking paper.

Roll the pastry out to 3-mm (⅛-in) thick on a lightly floured, clean bench. Cut out rounds using an 8-cm (3-in) pastry cutter. Brush the edges with egg white and place a small ball of date filling in the centre. Fold the pastry in half to enclose the filling and create a crescent shape. Press the curved edge with your finger tips to seal and place on the prepared tray.

Lightly brush the top of the crescents with egg white and bake in the oven for 15–20 minutes, until just golden. Transfer to a wire rack to cool.

Dust thoroughly with icing sugar and serve.

Almond Biscuits

Ghoriba

Makes 40

1¼ cups (200 g/7 oz) icing
   sugar, plus extra for dipping

1½ teaspoons baking powder

1 teaspoon ground cinnamon

360 g (13½ oz) ground
   almonds

3 large eggs, separated

1 tablespoon (20 g/¾ oz)
   butter, softened

finely grated zest of ½ lemon

Preheat the oven to 170°C (340°F). Lightly grease a baking tray.

Sift the icing sugar, baking powder and cinnamon together into a medium-sized bowl. Add the ground almonds and stir to combine.

Add the egg yolks, butter and lemon zest and stir to form a dough. Roll the dough into 40 even-sized balls and flatten slightly.

Lightly beat the egg whites in a small bowl. Dip the balls in egg white followed by icing sugar to coat.

Arrange the balls 2 cm (¾ in) apart on the prepared tray and bake in the oven for 15 minutes or until golden brown. Leave to cool on the tray for 10 minutes, then transfer to a wire rack to cool completely.

Macaroons

Makes 20

2½ cups whole almonds, plus
20 extra to decorate

1 cup (160 g/5½ oz) icing
sugar

1 teaspoon baking powder

½ teaspoon ground cinnamon

2 large eggs, separated

finely grated zest of ½ lemon

Preheat the oven to 180°C (360°F). Line a baking tray with baking paper.

Place the almonds in a food processor and blend until finely ground.

Combine the almonds, icing sugar, baking powder and cinnamon in a bowl. Add the egg yolks and lemon zest and rub together with your fingers to create a crumb-like texture.

Whip the egg whites in a bowl to form soft peaks. Add to the almond mixture and fold in gently to combine.

Shape the mixture into 20 even-sized balls. Arrange the macaroons roughly 2 cm (¾ in) apart on the prepared tray. Press an almond in the centre of each and flatten slightly. Bake in the oven for 15 minutes or until golden brown. Leave to cool on the tray for 10 minutes, then transfer to a wire rack to cool completely.

Moroccan Biscotti

Fekkas

Makes about 60

2½ cups (375 g/13 oz) plain
  flour

1 tablespoon (15 g/½ oz)
  baking powder

1 teaspoon ground cinnamon

1 cup (220 g/8 oz) caster sugar

3 large eggs

180 g (6½ oz) butter, melted

1 cup whole almonds, coarsely
  chopped

½ cup raisins

3 tablespoons sesame seeds

1 large egg white, lightly
  beaten

Preheat the oven to 180°C (360°F). Line a baking tray with baking paper.

Sift the flour, baking powder and cinnamon into a bowl.

Whisk the sugar and eggs together. Add the butter, almonds, raisins and
sesame seeds and stir to combine. Gradually add the flour, stirring until a
dough begins to form. Shape into two even-sized logs 5 cm (2 in) wide.
Transfer the logs to the prepared tray and brush the tops with egg white.
Bake for 20 minutes or until golden brown and firm to the touch.

Remove from the oven and set aside to cool for 20 minutes. Cut the logs,
using a sharp serrated knife, into 1-cm (⅜-in) thick slices. Return the slices
to the baking tray and bake for 10–15 minutes or until crisp and golden
brown. Remove from the oven and transfer to a wire rack to cool completely.

Semolina Biscuits with Dates

Makrout

Makes 30

vegetable oil, for deep-frying

DATE FILLING

250 g pitted dried dates

1 tablespoon (20 g/¾ oz) butter

1 tablespoon (20 ml/¾ fl oz) orange-blossom water

1 teaspoon ground cinnamon

DOUGH

1 cup (160 g/5½ oz) coarse semolina

1 cup (160 g/5½ oz) fine semolina

1 tablespoon (15 g/½ oz) caster sugar

pinch of salt

150 g (5 oz) butter, melted

¼ cup (60 ml/2 fl oz) orange-blossom water

HONEY DIP

1½ cups honey

1½ tablespoons (30 ml/1 fl oz) orange-blossom water

To make the filling, place the dates in a small saucepan with ¼ cup (60 ml/ 2 fl oz) water. Cover and cook over very low heat for 10 minutes, until softened. Set aside and allow to cool. Add the butter, orange-blossom water and cinnamon and stir to make a paste.

To make the dough, combine the semolinas, sugar and salt in a bowl. Add the butter, orange-blossom water and ⅓ cup (80 ml/3 fl oz) water and knead to form a dough. Shape the dough into a log. Make an incision down the centre line but not all the way through, leaving the log intact.

Shape the date filling into a log the same length as the dough log. Place the date log inside the incision and encase in the dough, pressing to seal. Score the top of the log in a decorative crisscross pattern and cut into 2 cm (¾ in) slices.

To make the honey dip, pour the honey and orange-blossom water into a medium-sized saucepan and warm over low heat.

Pour enough oil into a large frying pan for deep-frying. Heat oil to 180°C (360°F) or until a piece of bread browns in 15 seconds when tested.

Deep-fry the biscuits in batches for 1–2 minutes on each side, until golden brown and crisp. Remove using a slotted spoon, drain for a few seconds and place directly in the prepared honey dip. Hold down in the honey for 1 minute and turn until fully coated. Leave to soak up the honey for 1–2 minutes. Remove using a slotted spoon, allowing excess honey to drain. Place on a baking tray and set aside to cool.

Almond and Chocolate Slice

Zelliges

Makes 32

550 g (1 lb 3 oz) dark chocolate

210 g (8 oz) ground almonds

½ cup (80 g/3 oz) icing sugar

80 g (2¾ oz) butter, softened

50 g (1¾ oz) white chocolate

Line a 28-cm × 18-cm (11-in × 7-in) tray with baking paper.

Place the chocolate in a bowl and melt over a small saucepan of barely simmering water, stirring until smooth. Pour half of the chocolate into the prepared tray and, using a palate knife, spread out to an even layer. Refrigerate for 15–20 minutes, or until almost set.

Combine the ground almonds, icing sugar and butter in a bowl to form a paste. Roll out on a clean bench, lightly dusted with icing sugar, to a size to fit the chocolate-lined tray. Cut the almond paste into six large squares and lay over the chocolate base. Pour over the remaining dark chocolate and spread to create a smooth, even surface.

Melt the white chocolate using the method above. Drizzle back and forth over the dark chocolate to create a decorative pattern. Refrigerate for 15–20 minutes or until almost set. Mark the surface into 32 portions and refrigerate until set. Cut into portions using a hot knife.

Sweet Couscous

Serves 6

1½ cups couscous

1½ teaspoons salt

2 tablespoons (40 ml/1½ fl oz) vegetable oil

1 cup whole blanched almonds

½ cup raisins

80 g (3 oz) butter

½ cup (80 g/3 oz) icing sugar, plus extra, to serve (optional)

1 tablespoon ground cinnamon

chilled milk, to serve (optional)

Place the couscous in a large, wide-based tray or bowl. Combine 3 cups (750 ml/25 fl oz) water with the salt. Sprinkle 1 cup (250 ml/8 fl oz) of the salted water over the couscous, rubbing it through and separating the grains with your fingers as you go. Set aside for 10 minutes to allow the grains to swell with the water and dry out a little.

Fill the bottom of a steamer saucepan with water and bring to the boil. Rub your fingers through the couscous again, separating the grains. Place the couscous in the top of the steamer pan and set over the boiling water, ensuring that the top steamer section is not touching the water. When steam begins to rise through the couscous, steam for a further 10 minutes. Turn the couscous out onto a tray. Sprinkle with another 1 cup (250 ml/ 8 fl oz) salted water and rub through the couscous, separating the grains with your fingers. Set aside for 10 minutes to swell and dry out a little. **>**

Heat the oil in a medium-sized frying pan over low–medium heat. Add the almonds and cook until golden brown. Remove using a slotted spoon, drain on paper towel and coarsely chop.

Separate the couscous grains again using your fingers and return to the top of the steamer. When the steam begins to rise through the couscous, steam for a further 10 minutes. Tip the couscous back into the tray. Add the raisins and half of the butter, and sprinkle with the remaining salted water. Rub through the couscous, separating the grains with your fingers. Set aside for 10 minutes to swell and dry out a little.

Return the couscous to the steamer pan for one final steaming of 10 minutes. Tip the couscous back into the tray, add the remaining butter and mix through using your fingers to separate the grains.

Pile the couscous onto a serving dish to form a dome. To decorate, scatter with almonds and create alternate lines of icing sugar and cinnamon coming down from the centre point.

Serve with a drink of chilled milk, and sprinkle with additional icing sugar if desired.

Moroccan Rice Pudding

Serves 6–8

1⅓ cups short-grain rice

⅓ cup (75 g/2½ oz) sugar, plus extra to serve (optional)

½ teaspoon salt

1.25 L (2 pt 10 fl oz) milk

1 cinnamon stick

3 tablespoons (60 g/2 oz) butter

2 tablespoons (40 ml/1½ fl oz) orange-blossom water

2 teaspoons ground cinnamon

Place the rice, sugar and salt in a medium-sized saucepan with 2½ cups (625 ml/21 fl oz) water and bring to the boil. Decrease the heat to low and cook, stirring occasionally, until the water has been absorbed.

Add half of the milk, the cinnamon stick and half of the butter. Continue cooking on low, stirring occasionally to prevent the rice from sticking, until all the liquid has been absorbed. Gradually add the remaining milk, stirring until the rice is cooked and swollen and creamy in texture. Add the orange-blossom water. ❯

Spoon the rice onto a serving plate to form a dome shape. Decorate with lines of ground cinnamon coming down from the centre and dot with the remaining butter.

Serve with a drink of chilled milk, and additional sugar (if desired).

Sesame Brittle

Makes 30

1 cup (220 g/8 oz) caster sugar
1 cup sesame seeds, toasted

Place the sugar in a small saucepan over low heat. Heat until it begins to melt and turn golden. Swirl the sugar around so that it colours evenly, but do not stir. When it turns a light golden colour, add the sesame seeds, swirling to combine and evenly distribute.

Pour out onto an oiled marble or metal surface. Using a lightly oiled rolling pin or metal spoon, spread out the toffee to make a 5-mm (¼-in) thick square. Work quickly or the toffee will harden. Set aside for 5 minutes to harden completely.

Cut into approximately 30 squares.

Store in a dry airtight container for up to 2 weeks.

Stuffed Dates

Makes 20

80 g (3 oz) ground almonds

2 tablespoons (20 g/¾ oz) icing sugar

½ teaspoon ground cinnamon

2 teaspoons orange-blossom water

few drops of green food colouring

few drops of pink food colouring

20 fresh dates, pitted

caster sugar, for sprinkling

Combine the ground almonds, icing sugar and cinnamon in a small bowl. Gradually add the orange-blossom water and blend to create a paste. Divide the paste in half.

Tint half of the paste pale green and the other half pale pink, adding a few drops at a time of the appropriate food colouring and stirring to combine.

Shape the filling into small rounded logs and stuff inside the dates. Sprinkle with caster sugar and arrange on a serving plate.

Sesame, Almond & Honey Cone

Slelou

Makes 2 cups

2⅓ cups (350 g/12 oz) plain
  flour

2 cups whole blanched
  almonds

240 g (8½ oz) sesame seeds

225 g (8 oz) butter, melted

3 tablespoons honey

½ cup (80 g/3 oz) icing sugar,
  plus extra for dusting

2 teaspoons ground cinnamon

1 teaspoon ground aniseed

¼ teaspoon ground nutmeg

2 tablespoons (40 ml/1½ fl oz)
  vegetable oil

Toast the flour in a dry frying pan over low heat, stirring constantly, until golden brown. Transfer to a medium-sized bowl and set aside to cool.

Toast 1½ cups almonds and the sesame seeds in the same frying pan, over low heat, until golden brown. Set aside to cool.

Melt the butter and honey together in a small saucepan over low heat. Set aside to cool slightly.

Transfer the almonds and sesame seeds to a food processor and blend to a fine powder. Add the toasted flour, icing sugar, cinnamon, aniseed and nutmeg and blend until combined. Transfer to a medium-sized bowl. Pour in the honey and butter mixture and stir to combine. >

Heat the oil in a medium-sized frying pan over low heat. Add the remaining almonds and fry until golden. Remove using a slotted spoon, drain on paper towel and set aside to cool.

Pile the almond and sesame mixture into a cone shape on a serving plate and dust heavily with icing sugar. Decorate with the whole almonds, creating three or four lines coming down from the centre point.

* Slelou is served as a celebratory dish at weddings and after a child has been born. It is also offered during Ramadan to restore energy and provide nourishment. Slelou is traditionally eaten communally with teaspoons.

* Instead of making a cone shape with the mixture, add 2 extra tablespoons of honey and shape the mixture into small balls. Roll in icing sugar and decorate each ball with half a toasted almond.

Fresh Figs with Honey & Toasted Almonds

Serves 4

2 tablespoons flaked almonds

8 ripe fresh figs

1 tablespoon fragrant runny honey

Preheat a grill to medium–high.

Spread the almonds over a baking tray and toast under the grill until golden.

Cut the figs in half lengthways and arrange on a serving plate. Drizzle with the honey and scatter with the toasted almonds.

Serve immediately.

Cinnamon-spiced Orange Slices

Serves 4

4 oranges

1 tablespoon (20 ml/¾ fl oz)
  orange-blossom water

1 teaspoon ground cinnamon

Peel the oranges using a small sharp knife and cut away the pith. Slice the oranges into rounds, removing any seeds.

Arrange the orange slices on a serving plate. Drizzle with the orange-blossom water and sprinkle with the cinnamon.

Serve immediately.

Melon & Mint Salad

Serves 4–6

¼ **small watermelon**

¼ **honeydew (green) melon**

¼ **cantaloupe (orange) melon**

3 **tablespoons finely chopped
fresh mint**

Remove and discard the skin of the watermelon and cut into 4-cm (1½-in) cubes. Remove and discard any visible seeds.

Remove and discard the skins off the remaining melons, scoop out and discard the seeds and cut into 4-cm (1½-in) cubes.

Place the melon and mint in a large bowl and toss to combine.

Serve immediately.

Breads, Drinks & Extras

Moroccan cuisine would not be the same without the delicious extras that follow. Try making Moroccan bread so you can eat tagine the traditional way, with your right hand, soaking up the juices as you go. And with your own preserved lemons, harissa, ras el hanout and marinated olives in the kitchen, you'll never be short of ways to add flavour to tagines, fish and meat dishes.

A traditional Moroccan breakfast is a great way to start the day. Recipes here include harchas, m'smmens and beghrir topped with amalou, jam, or melted butter and fragrant honey.

Sweetened mint tea is a part of daily life in Morocco. It is served after most meals, sipped throughout the day, shared as a part of making business deals and always made when visitors stop by. Prepared before you in ceremonial fashion, the tea is boiled, poured, discarded and re-poured into small, intricately decorated glasses.

< Semolina Flatbread (page 222)

Semolina Flatbread

Harchas

Makes 1

1½ cups (240 g/8½ oz) fine
semolina, plus extra for
sprinkling

1 tablespoon (15 g/½ oz) caster
sugar

1 teaspoon baking powder

½ teaspoon salt

1 cup (250 ml/8½ fl oz) milk

Combine the semolina, sugar, baking powder and salt in a medium-sized bowl. Add the milk, stir to combine and set aside for 5 minutes.

Preheat a medium-sized non-stick frying pan over low–medium heat. Sprinkle the pan with semolina. Spoon the mixture into the pan and press down flat using a wet hand. Sprinkle with semolina and cook for 3–5 minutes on each side until golden brown.

Cut in half horizontally around the circumference (as you would an English muffin).

Serve warm with butter and honey, jam or amalou (page 230).

Moroccan Crêpes

M'smmens

Makes 8

160 g (5½ oz) fine semolina,
   plus extra for sprinkling

3 cups (450 g/1 lb) plain flour

2 teaspoons baking powder

2 tablespoons (30 g/1 oz)
   caster sugar

1 teaspoon salt

125 g (4½ oz) unsalted butter

vegetable oil, for frying

Sift the semolina, flour, baking powder, sugar and salt into a medium-sized bowl. Gradually add 1 cup (250 ml/8½ fl oz) water, stirring to combine until a dough begins to form. Knead the dough for 10 minutes or until a smooth, elastic ball is formed. Set aside for 10 minutes to rest.

Meanwhile, melt the butter in a small saucepan over low heat and set aside.

Using lightly oiled hands, shape the dough into eight balls, approximately twice the size of golfballs. Flatten the balls out one at a time into 15-cm (6-in) discs. Drizzle with melted butter and lightly sprinkle with semolina. Fold the edges into the centre, overlapping to make a rectangle. Half-turn and fold the edges in again, overlapping to make a small square parcel. Set aside to rest for 10 minutes. >

Flatten each dough parcel into a square about the size of your hand.

Heat a medium-sized frying pan over medium–high heat. Drizzle with oil and cook the squares for 10 seconds on each side to seal. Cook for a further 1–2 minutes on each side, until golden.

Serve hot with butter and honey, jam or amalou (page 230).

❊ M'smmens are a traditional Moroccan breakfast food.

Moroccan Bread

Makes 3 × 10-cm (4-in) round loaves

2½ cups (375 g/13 oz) plain flour

1 cup (145 g/5 oz) wholemeal flour

2 teaspoons salt

1 tablespoon (15 g/½ oz) dry yeast

1 tablespoon (15 g/½ oz) sugar

1¼ cups (310 ml/10½ fl oz) lukewarm water

fine semolina, for sprinkling

Sift the flours and salt together into a large bowl and make a well in the centre. Place the yeast and sugar in the well. Pour ½ cup (125 ml/4 fl oz) water into the well, mixing with the yeast to combine. Gradually add the remaining water and stir in the flour until a dough begins to form.

Knead the dough for 10–15 minutes, adding a little extra water or flour if necessary, to make a smooth, elastic dough. Divide the dough into three equal-sized balls and place on a lightly greased tray. Cover with a clean tea towel and put in a warm place for 30–45 minutes, until doubled in size.

Meanwhile, preheat the oven to 200°C–220°C (390°F–420°F). Lightly oil 2 large baking trays and sprinkle with fine semolina. **>**

Using the palm of your hand, press and flatten the balls out to 10-cm (4-in) discs. Sprinkle the tops with semolina and transfer to the prepared baking trays. Bake in the oven for 15–20 minutes or until golden brown. When the bread is cooked it will sound hollow when tapped on the base.

❋ Bread is eaten at almost every Moroccan meal. It is used to soak up the juices of tagine and to scoop tasty morsels into your mouth.

❋ As this bread contains no preservatives, it is best eaten on the day it is made.

Semolina Pancakes

Beghrir

Makes 30

3½ cups (875 ml/29½ fl oz)
lukewarm water

2½ teaspoons (10 g/⅜ oz) dry
yeast

600 g (1 lb 5 oz) fine semolina

¾ cup (110 g/4 oz) plain flour

1 tablespoon (15 g/½ oz)
baking powder

2 teaspoons salt

1 tablespoon (20 ml/¾ fl oz)
orange-blossom water

Combine ⅓ cup (80 ml/3 fl oz) water and the yeast in a small bowl.

Sift the semolina, flour, baking powder and salt into a large bowl. Make a well in the dry ingredients and add the yeast mixture, remaining water and orange-blossom water, and stir to combine.

Pour the semolina mixture into a food processor and blend for 2–3 minutes, to create a smooth, cream-like consistency. Transfer to a large bowl, cover with a clean tea towel and set aside in a warm place for 20–30 minutes, until bubbly.

Preheat a small non-stick frying pan over medium–high heat. Pour a small ladleful of batter into the pan and slightly rotate the pan to create an even disc. Turn the heat down to medium and cook on one side for 1–2 minutes, until the bubbles have popped and the pancake has cooked through. Remove from the pan using a palette knife or egg flip and set aside under a clean tea towel to keep warm.

Repeat with the remaining mixture.

Serve warm with butter and honey, jam or amalou (page 230).

❉ Beghrir are a traditional Moroccan breakfast food. They can be frozen for future use.

Almond & Honey Spread

Amalou

Makes about 1 cup

160 g (6 oz) ground almonds

**⅓ cup (80 ml/3 fl oz) walnut or
vegetable oil**

3 tablespoons honey

Place the ground almonds in a large frying pan over low–medium heat and toast for 4–5 minutes, until golden brown. Combine with the oil and honey in a small bowl and mix well. Add more honey for sweetness, if desired.

❄ Serve amalou with Moroccan bread (page 225), beghrir (page 228) or m'smmens (page 223).

❄ Amalou will keep in a sealed jar in the refrigerator for 2–3 weeks.

Broad Bean Purée

Makes about 2 cups

1¼ cups dried broad beans

3 cloves garlic

3 cups (750 ml/25 fl oz) water

¼ cup (60 ml/2 fl oz) extra-
   virgin olive oil

salt

paprika, for garnish

ground cumin, for garnish

Soak the broad beans in cold water for at least 6 hours or overnight. Drain, rinse and skin the beans.

Place the beans and garlic in a medium-sized saucepan and cover with the water. Bring to the boil, then decrease the heat and gently simmer for 1–1½ hours, until the beans are soft.

Purée the beans in a food processor. Add the olive oil and stir to combine. Season with salt.

Place in a serving dish and sprinkle with paprika and cumin. Serve warm or cold with bread.

Harissa Paste

Makes ¾ cup

40 g (1½ oz) dried red chillies

4 cloves garlic, coarsely
   chopped

1 teaspoon ground coriander

1 teaspoon ground cumin

¼ teaspoon salt

2 tablespoons (40 ml/1½ fl oz)
   olive oil

Place the chillies in a medium-sized bowl and cover with boiling water. Leave to soak for 1 hour. Drain and coarsely chop.

Place the chillies, garlic, coriander, cumin and salt in a food processor and blend for 10 seconds. Continue blending and gradually add the oil in a thin stream until the mixture forms a paste.

Place the harissa in a clean, airtight jar and cover with a thin layer of oil. Store in the refrigerator.

❋ Use harissa to marinate meat, poultry or fish, or add it to dressings for a spicier flavour.

❋ Harissa will keep for 2–3 months in the refrigerator.

Chermoula Paste

Makes ¾ cup (180 ml/6 fl oz)

3 cloves garlic, chopped

½ bunch fresh coriander, leaves chopped

½ bunch fresh flat-leaf parsley, leaves chopped

¼ cup (60 ml/2 fl oz) olive oil

¼ cup (60 ml/2 fl oz) lemon juice

1½ teaspoons paprika

1 teaspoon ground cumin

1 teaspoon ground coriander

½ teaspoon freshly ground black pepper

½ teaspoon salt

Place the garlic, coriander and parsley in a food processor and blend to a paste. Add the olive oil, lemon juice, spices and salt and blend to combine.

❋ Chermoula is traditionally used to marinate fish and seafood.

❋ Store chermoula in the fridge for 2–3 days in an airtight container, covered with a thin layer of oil.

Preserved Lemons

Makes 10–12

10–12 unwaxed lemons

¾ cup (165 g/5½ oz) coarse
sea salt

½ teaspoon black peppercorns

2 bay leaves

¼ cup (60 ml/2 fl oz) lemon
juice

Preheat the oven to 120°C (240°F). Sterilise a large, 2-L (4-pt 4-fl oz) capacity preserving jar with boiling water and dry out thoroughly in the oven.

Scrub the lemons and rinse well under cold running water.

Cut the lemons in quarters lengthways, leaving the bases intact. Separate the lemon quarters, salt the insides and rejoin. Pack the lemons, base first to prevent the salt from falling out, into the prepared preserving jar. Scatter with the peppercorns and bay leaves and pour in the lemon juice. Pour in enough boiling water to almost fill the jar. Place a piece of baking paper on top of the lemons and weigh this down with something heavy to keep them submerged. Seal the jar and store in a dark place for 1–4 months.

Upon opening, remove and discard the baking paper and any white film that has formed on top. Store in the refrigerator.

✼ When using preserved lemons, generally the flesh and membrane is removed and discarded. Rinse the skin and add to tagines and salads. The preserving liquid can be kept and re-used to make your next batch.

Marinated Olives

Serves 4–6

½ preserved lemon, quartered, flesh discarded and skin finely sliced lengthways

2 cups green olives, rinsed

1 cup kalamata olives, rinsed

½ cup (125 ml/4 fl oz) olive oil

2 tablespoons (40 ml/1½ fl oz) lemon juice

2 tablespoons finely chopped fresh flat-leaf parsley

2 tablespoons finely chopped fresh coriander

1 red chilli, deseeded and finely sliced

1 clove garlic, finely sliced

1 teaspoon ground cumin

Place all the ingredients in a medium-sized bowl and stir to combine. Cover and place in the refrigerator for 1–2 days to marinate.

Serve warmed or at room temperature.

Spiced Coffee Mix

Makes 12 cups coffee

2 teaspoons ground ginger

1 teaspoon ground nutmeg

1 teaspoon ground cardamom

1 teaspoon ground cinnamon

½ teaspoon ground aniseed

½ teaspoon ground cloves

½ teaspoon freshly ground
   black pepper

Combine all the spices in a small bowl.

To prepare a drink of spiced coffee, combine ¼ teaspoon of spice mix per cup of coffee with your coffee grounds. Prepare the coffee in your usual way, using a plunger or percolator. Refer to manufacturer's instructions if necessary.

❋ You can store this spiced coffee mix in an airtight container in a cool, dark place for up to 2 months.

Spice Mix

Ras el hanout

Makes 4 tablespoons

3 teaspoons ground nutmeg

2 teaspoons ground cumin

2 teaspoons ground ginger

2 teaspoons freshly ground
black pepper

1 teaspoon ground coriander

1 teaspoon ground allspice

1 teaspoon ground cardamom

½ teaspoon ground turmeric

½ teaspoon cayenne pepper

¼ teaspoon ground cloves

Combine all the spices in a small bowl.

❋ Ras el hanout is a traditional spice mix containing 10 or more spices. Combinations are as varied as the makers. It is used to flavour tagines, couscous and bastilla.

❋ Store in an airtight container in a cool, dark place for up to 2 months.

Almond Milk

Serves 4–6

2 cups whole blanched
  almonds

½ cup (110 g/4 oz) caster sugar

3 cups (750 ml/25 fl oz) milk,
  chilled

2 teaspoons orange-blossom
  water

Place the almonds and sugar in a food processor and blend to make a coarse crumb-like consistency. Add 1 cup (250 ml/8½ fl oz) water and blend for a further minute. Transfer to a large jar and set aside for 30 minutes to soak.

Add the milk and orange-blossom water to the almond mixture and pass through a fine strainer.

Serve chilled immediately, or as a snack between meals.

Avocado Drink

Serves 2

1 ripe avocado, pitted

½ cup ice cubes

2 pitted fresh dates, coarsely
chopped

1 tablespoon (15 g/½ oz) caster
sugar

2 cups (500 ml/17 fl oz) milk,
chilled

Scoop out the flesh of the avocado and place in a food processor. Add the ice cubes, dates and sugar and blend for 30 seconds. Add half of the milk and blend for a further 30 seconds, until smooth. Add the remaining milk and blend to combine.

Serve chilled immediately, or as a snack between meals.

Peach Milkshake

Sharbat

Serves 4

2 large ripe peaches

2 cups (500 ml/17 fl oz) chilled milk

½ cup (125 ml/4 fl oz) iced water

2 tablespoons (30 g/1 oz) caster sugar

½ teaspoon rosewater

ground cinnamon, for sprinkling

Score a cross at the base of the peaches. Bring a pot of water to the boil and blanch the peaches quickly, then plunge into iced water. Peel and discard the skin from the peaches, and roughly chop the flesh.

Put the peach and the remaining ingredients in a blender or food processor, and blend until combined well.

Pour into chilled glasses and sprinkle with a little cinnamon to serve.

Moroccan Mint Tea

Serves 2–3

1 tablespoon Chinese
  gunpowder green tea

6 sprigs fresh spearmint

3–4 sugar cubes (or to taste)

2 cups (500 ml/17 fl oz) boiling
  water

Place the tea in a medium-sized teapot (capacity about 500 ml/ 17 fl oz) suitable for the stovetop and just cover with water. Set over low–medium heat and bring to the boil. Discard the water but retain the tea in the teapot. Refill the teapot with fresh water to three-quarters full, return to the heat and bring to the boil. Remove from the heat, add the mint and sugar and set aside to steep for 3 minutes.

Pour some tea into two small glasses, then return it to the teapot (this helps to combine the flavours). Taste the tea for sweetness and add more sugar if desired. Serve in small tea glasses, poured from a height to aerate.

❋ The Moroccan tea ceremony is preformed in front of guests. The tea is boiled, poured, discarded, and re-poured always from a height.

❋ Other herbs, such as thyme, can be used to make Moroccan tea, but spearmint is the most widely used. Either fresh or dried mint can be used depending on availability and individual taste.

Special Ingredients

AMALOU This almond and honey spread is easy to make and keeps for up to three weeks.

CHERMOULA A dry spice mix traditionally used to marinate fish and seafood. It can be purchased from specialist food stores.

CHINESE GUNPOWDER TEA A green tea of granular appearance. The tightly rolled leaves have a refreshing taste, especially when added to preparations for Moroccan mint tea.

HARISSA A chilli-hot sauce used to flavour many Moroccan dishes. It can be easily made or purchased from most supermarkets.

MARSHMALLOW LEAVES Readily available at Moroccan markets when in season, they can be difficult to find outside of Morocco. Spinach is an appropriate substitute.

ORANGE-BLOSSOM WATER (orange-flower water) A solution of orange-blossom oil in water. Used mainly as a flavouring in desserts.

PRESERVED LEMONS When using preserved lemons, generally the pulp and membrane are removed and discarded. Rinse the skin and add to tagines and salads.

RAS EL HANOUT A Middle Eastern spice mix containing 10 or more spices. Combinations are as varied as the makers. The recipes in this book use the blend common to Moroccan cooking on page 242. Ready-made versions can be purchased from most supermarkets.

ROSEWATER A scented water made with rose petals, used to add a distinctive aroma and flavour to food, especially sweets.

SAFFRON A small amount of saffron threads is enough to add brilliant yellow colour, delicate fragrance and distinctive flavour.

WARKA PASTRY A paper-thin Moroccan pastry sold in large rounds resembling crêpes. It is used in Moroccan cooking to make dishes such as bastilla and briouats. For frying, spring-roll wrappers make a good substitute. For baking, filo is more suitable – spring-roll wrappers tend to become rubbery when baked.

Conversions

Important note: All cup and spoon measures given in this book are based on Australian standards. The most important thing to remember is that an Australian cup = 250 ml, while an American cup = 237 ml and a British cup = 284 ml. Also, an Australian tablespoon is equivalent to 4 teaspoons, not 3 teaspoons as in the United States and Britain. US equivalents have been provided throughout for all liquid cup/spoon measures. Equivalents for dry ingredients measured in cups/spoons have been included for flour, sugar and rising agents such as baking powder. For other dry ingredients (chopped vegetables, nuts, etc.), American cooks should be generous with their cup measures – slight variations in quantities of such ingredients are unlikely to affect results.

VOLUME

Australian cups/spoons	Millilitres	US fluid ounces
* 1 teaspoon	5 ml	
1 tablespoon (4 teaspoons)	20 ml	¾ fl oz
1½ tablespoons	30 ml	1 fl oz
2 tablespoons	40 ml	1½ fl oz
¼ cup	60 ml	2 fl oz
⅓ cup	80 ml	3 fl oz
½ cup	125 ml	4 fl oz
¾ cup	180 ml	6 fl oz
1 cup	250 ml	8½ fl oz
4 cups	1 L	34 fl oz

*the volume of a teaspoon is the same around the world

SIZE

Centimetres	Inches
1 cm	⅜ in
2 cm	¾ in
2.5 cm	1 in
5 cm	2 in
10 cm	4 in
15 cm	6 in
20 cm	8 in
30 cm	12 in

TEMPERATURE

Celsius	Fahrenheit
150°C	300°F
160°C	320°F
170°C	340°F
180°C	360°F
190°C	375°F
200°C	390°F
210°C	410°F
220°C	420°F

WEIGHT

Grams	Ounces
15 g	½ oz
30 g	1 oz
60 g	2 oz
85 g	3 oz
110 g	4 oz
140 g	5 oz
170 g	6 oz
200 g	7 oz
225 g	8 oz (½ lb)
450 g	16 oz (1 lb)
500 g	1 lb 2 oz
900 g	2 lb
1 kg	2 lb 3 oz

Index